D0041261

THE AMERICAN PRESIDENTS SERIES

Joyce Appleby on *Thomas Jefferson*
Louis Auchincloss on *Theodore Roosevelt*
Jean Baker on *James Buchanan*
H. W. Brands on *Woodrow Wilson*
Douglas Brinkley on *Gerald Ford*
James MacGregor Burns and Susan Dunn on *George Washington*
Robert Dallek on *James Monroe*
John W. Dean on *Warren Harding*
John Patrick Diggins on *John Adams*
E. L. Doctorow on *Abraham Lincoln*
Henry F. Graff on *Grover Cleveland*
Roy Jenkins on *Franklin Delano Roosevelt*
Zachary Karabell on *Chester A. Arthur*
William E. Leuchtenburg on *Herbert Hoover*
Robert V. Remini on *John Quincy Adams*
John Seigenthaler on *James K. Polk*
Hans L. Trefousse on *Rutherford B. Hayes*
Tom Wicker on *Dwight D. Eisenhower*
Ted Widmer on *Martin Van Buren*
Sean Wilentz on *Andrew Jackson*
Garry Wills on *James Madison*

*The Devil We Knew: Americans and the Cold War*

*TR: The Last Romantic*

*What America Owes the World:*
*The Struggle for the Soul of Foreign Policy*

*The First American: The Life and Times of Benjamin Franklin*

*The Age of Gold:*
*The California Gold Rush and the New American Dream*

# Woodrow
# Wilson

# H. W. Brands

# Woodrow Wilson

### THE AMERICAN PRESIDENTS

ARTHUR M. SCHLESINGER, JR., GENERAL EDITOR

Times Books

HENRY HOLT AND COMPANY, NEW YORK

Times Books
Henry Holt and Company, LLC
*Publishers since 1866*
115 West 18th Street
New York, New York 10011

Henry Holt® is a registered trademark of Henry Holt and Company, LLC.

LIBRARY OF CONGRESS CATALOGING-IN-PUBLICATION DATA
Brands, H. W.
    Woodrow Wilson / H. W. Brands.—1st ed.
    p. cm.—(The American presidents)
    Includes bibliographical references (p. ) and index.
    ISBN: 0-8050-6955-0
        1. Wilson, Woodrow, 1856–1924.  2. Presidents—United States—
    Biography. 3. United States—Politics and government—1913–1921.
    I. Title. II. American presidents series (Times Books (Firm))
    E767.B76 2003
    973.91'3'092–dc21
    [B}                                                                  2002041393

First Edition 2003

Printed in the United States of America
1  3  5  7  9  10  8  6  4  2

# Contents

*Editor's Note*                                    xiii

1. To See the Benches Smile                          1
2. The Irony of Fate                                41
3. More Precious than Peace                         73
4. What We Dreamed at Our Birth                     99
5. Provincials No Longer                           131

*Notes*                                            141
*Milestones*                                       149
*Selected Bibliography*                            153
*Index*                                            157

# Editor's Note

The president is the central player in the American political order. That would seem to contradict the intentions of the Founding Fathers. Remembering the horrid example of the British monarchy, they invented a separation of powers in order, as Justice Brandeis later put it, "to preclude the exercise of arbitrary power." Accordingly, they divided the government into three allegedly equal and coordinate branches—the executive, the legislative, and the judiciary.

But a system based on the tripartite separation of powers has an inherent tendency toward inertia and stalemate. One of the three branches must take the initiative if the system is to move. The executive branch alone is structurally capable of taking that initiative. The Founders must have sensed this when they accepted Alexander Hamilton's proposition in the Seventieth Federalist that "energy in the executive is a leading character in the definition of good government." They thus envisaged a strong president—but within an equally strong system of constitutional accountability. (The term *imperial presidency* arose in the 1970s to describe the situation when the balance between power and accountability is upset in favor of the executive.)

The American system of self-government thus comes to focus in the presidency—"the vital place of action in the system," as Woodrow Wilson put it. Henry Adams, himself the great-grandson and grandson of presidents as well as the most brilliant of American historians, said that the American president "resembles the commander of a ship at sea. He must have a helm to grasp, a course to steer, a port to seek." The men in the White House (thus far only men, alas) in steering their chosen courses have shaped our destiny as a nation.

Biography offers an easy education in American history, rendering the past more human, more vivid, more intimate, more accessible, more connected to ourselves. Biography reminds us that presidents are not supermen. They are human beings too, worrying about decisions, attending to wives and children, juggling balls in the air, and putting on their pants one leg at a time. Indeed, as Emerson contended, "There is properly no history; only biography."

Presidents serve us as inspirations, and they also serve us as warnings. They provide bad examples as well as good. The nation, the Supreme Court has said, has "no right to expect that it will always have wise and humane rulers, sincerely attached to the principles of the Constitution. Wicked men, ambitious of power, with hatred of liberty and contempt of law, may fill the place once occupied by Washington and Lincoln."

The men in the White House express the ideal and the values, the frailties and the flaws, of the voters who send them there. It is altogether natural that we should want to know more about the virtues and the vices of the fellows we have elected to govern us. As we know more about them, we will know more about ourselves. The French political philosopher Joseph de Maistre said, "Every nation has the government it deserves."

At the start of the twenty-first century, forty-two men have made it to the Oval Office. (George W. Bush is counted our forty-third president, because Grover Cleveland, who served nonconsecutive terms, is counted twice.) Of the parade of presidents, a dozen or so lead the polls periodically conducted by historians and political scientists. What makes a great president?

Great presidents possess, or are possessed by, a vision of an ideal America. Their passion, as they grasp the helm, is to set the ship of state on the right course toward the port they seek. Great presidents also have a deep psychic connection with the needs, anxieties, dreams of people. "I do not believe," said Wilson, "that any man can lead who does not act . . . under the impulse of a profound sympathy with those whom he leads—a sympathy which is insight—an insight which is of the heart rather than of the intellect."

"All of our great presidents," said Franklin D. Roosevelt, "were leaders of thought at a time when certain ideas in the life of the nation had to be clarified." So Washington incarnated the idea of federal union, Jefferson and Jackson the idea of democracy, Lincoln union and freedom, Cleveland rugged honesty. Theodore Roosevelt and Wilson, said FDR, were both "moral leaders, each in his own way and his own time, who used the presidency as a pulpit."

To succeed, presidents must not only have a port to seek but they must convince Congress and the electorate that it is a port worth seeking. Politics in a democracy is ultimately an educational process, an adventure in persuasion and consent. Every president stands in Theodore Roosevelt's bully pulpit.

The greatest presidents in the scholars' rankings, Washington, Lincoln, and Franklin Roosevelt, were leaders who confronted and overcame the republic's greatest crises. Crisis widens presidential opportunities for bold and imaginative action. But it does not guarantee presidential greatness. The crisis of secession did not spur Buchanan or the crisis of depression spur Hoover to creative leadership. Their inadequacies in the face of crisis allowed Lincoln and the second Roosevelt to show the difference individuals make to history. Still, even in the absence of first-order crisis, forceful and persuasive presidents—Jackson, Theodore Roosevelt, Ronald Reagan—are able to impose their own priorities on the country.

The diverse drama of the presidency offers a fascinating set of tales. Biographies of American presidents constitute a chronicle of wisdom and folly, nobility and pettiness, courage and cunning, forthrightness and deceit, quarrel and consensus. The turmoil perennially swirling around the White House illuminates the heart of the American democracy.

It is the aim of the American Presidents series to present the grand panorama of our chief executives in volumes compact enough for the busy reader, lucid enough for the student, authoritative enough for the scholar. Each volume offers a distillation of character and career. I hope that these lives will give readers some understanding of the pitfalls and potentialities of the presidency and also of the responsibilities of citizenship. Truman's famous sign—"The buck stops here"—tells only half the story. Citizens cannot escape the ultimate responsibility. It is in the voting booth, not on the presidential desk, that the buck finally stops.

—Arthur M. Schlesinger, Jr.

# Woodrow Wilson

# 1

## To See the Benches Smile

In the beginning was the word. And in the end was the word. And in between were words: beautiful words, soaring words, words that moved a nation and enthralled a world, words that for a wonderful moment were more powerful than armies, words that made the most terrible sacrifice seem part of a glorious struggle, words that echoed across the oceans and down the decades.

Woodrow Wilson was a man of words. His actions weren't insignificant: he guided America onto a new plateau of social responsibility, and he led the nation to victory in a terrible war. But his legacy was his words, and though his steps faltered at his journey's end, his words lived on, inspiring later generations to achieve what he never could.

Wilson was from the South by way of the North, which went far toward explaining how he won the Democratic nomination for president in 1912. His forebears hadn't been long in America, with his mother an immigrant and his father the son of immigrants. Scots predominated in his ancestry, although some kin had relocated to the north of Ireland, allowing Wilson to claim

Irish lineage when convenient. His father grew up in Ohio, where he met Wilson's mother, who had narrowly escaped being swept overboard by a rogue wave en route from Liverpool. The couple married in 1849, two weeks before Joseph Wilson's ordination as a Presbyterian minister. They remained in Ohio long enough to have two daughters, but in 1854 a better pulpit became available in western Virginia, in the Blue Ridge town of Staunton. There Thomas Woodrow Wilson was born on December 28, 1856.

Yet Tommy, as the boy was called, never knew Staunton, at least not to remember. In 1858 the ambitious Reverend Wilson found another church, in Augusta, Georgia. At a time when the issue of slavery had grown explosively sensitive, Joseph Wilson followed many of his southern colleagues-in-the-cloth in discovering biblical sanction for the peculiar institution. The Bible had less to say about secession, when that came, but Joseph Wilson had no difficulty rendering Caesar—or Jefferson Davis—his due. During the Civil War, Wilson served briefly in the Confederate army before returning to his flock.

Had the Wilson family lived in Atlanta or on the route of Sherman's march to the sea, the war would have had a deeper influence on young Tommy. But Augusta was comparatively sheltered, and the conflict often seemed something that happened to other people. This impression grew stronger in retrospect, for after the southern surrender, the northern roots of the family, combined with Joseph Wilson's religious calling, protected the household from the harsher aspects of Reconstruction.

Yet perhaps Tommy wouldn't have noticed the revolutionary events of the war and its aftermath even if Sherman himself had burned the Wilson house down. In youth he displayed an uncanny ability to view life as if from outside. Later, speaking of children generally but almost certainly extrapolating from his own experience, he characterized the typical child as standing "upon a place apart, a little spectator of the world."[1] Referring specifically to his own childhood, he said, "I lived a dream life."[2]

The dreams of another Civil War child—Theodore Roosevelt, who experienced the conflict from the relatively safe distance of New York City and whose life path would intersect Wilson's significantly—were filled with literary adventure, with tales of the heroes of history and romance. But not Tommy Wilson's, for the boy in Georgia didn't learn to read until he was ten years old. A later generation of pediatricians and educators likely would have diagnosed dyslexia, but in Tommy's time the boy just seemed slow. Had he been of a different family, he might have turned his back on the land of letters; but with a father whose vocation depended on translating the Word of God into the words of men, and who, by the evidence of every Sunday, excelled in the art, Tommy couldn't help being drawn in. He perceived letters and words as possessing a mysterious power, a power not easily captured and the more potent for its elusiveness and mystery. When he finally did decode the alphabet and enter the priesthood of the literate, he felt an exhilaration that stayed with him his whole life.

At fourteen the family moved again, to Columbia, South Carolina. The Reverend Wilson was appointed professor of pastoral theology at the Presbyterian seminary there, a position he supplemented by service as interim minister of the First Presbyterian Church. Tommy received tutoring from one of the seminary's professors. Though his academic progress continued slowly, he became enamored of a system of shorthand he saw advertised in a magazine. The ads touted the time-saving features of the system—an obscure variant of the more popular systems of the day—for secretaries and stenographers, its obvious clientele. What doubtless intrigued young Wilson was its very obscurity. Having been so long mastering ordinary letters, Wilson by this leap could surpass that large majority of writers to whom the unusual system was not vouchsafed. (Although he couldn't know it at the time, he thereby complicated the labors of future archivists and editors who, in processing his papers, had to decipher the hieroglyphics of the long-forgotten system.) The leap was a struggle; the young man required years to attain proficiency. But he evidently thought the prize worth the toil, for he soldiered on.

At seventeen Tommy left home to pursue his education. He attended Davidson College of North Carolina, which was not so far away as to rule out occasional visits home, nor so selective as to prevent the admission of a student whose performance still lagged many of his peers', nor so secular as to eliminate the possibility of the son's following the father's footsteps.

His classroom work improved, especially in the humanities. He discovered an interest in history and, to his surprise, a talent for writing. He also discovered a passion for public speaking. He joined the debating club and devoured the library's collection on rhetorical technique and great speakers of the past.

Davidson, however, proved a false start. Tommy stayed one year, toward the end of which his father moved yet again. Doctrinal disputes and financial troubles forced the Columbia seminary to close and the Reverend Wilson to find another job, which he did in Wilmington, North Carolina. Had Tommy been more enamored of Davidson, the strain on the family budget caused by the job switch and the household move might not have forced his withdrawal from the college; but as it was, he decided that a suspension of his higher education was in the family's and his own interest. (The Wilson family's finances inspired a story often told about the Reverend Wilson. When someone remarked that the minister's horse was better groomed than the minister, Dr. Wilson replied, "That is because I care for my horse. My parishioners care for me.")[3]

Tommy Wilson spent the next year in Wilmington, polishing his shorthand, observing the arrivals and departures of ships in the harbor, reading the novels of Walter Scott, and wondering what life held for him. Yet one thing he knew, as he told a friend from Davidson: "I like nothing so well as writing and talking."[4]

During this period the idea of going north to college took shape in his head. Dr. Wilson, who had attended seminary in Princeton, New Jersey, knew the man who currently headed the College of New Jersey, commonly called Princeton, located in the same town. The college lacked the reputation to draw all the students its upkeep required, and its president, on one of his recruiting and fund-raising trips through the Carolinas, cast his eye on the son of his old friend. After a year under the parental roof, Tommy was ready to leave again, and in September 1875, three months before his nineteenth birthday, he boarded a northbound train.

He entered the life of the college with some diffidence. He joined one of the newer eating clubs, the Alligators, and played on the freshman baseball team. But his classes were uninspiring. "Study review in Xenophon's Memorabilia for examinations all the afternoon and evening," he jotted in the diary he kept in shorthand. "Very stupid work." Two days later he wrote, "Studied geometry from 8 to 10—very stupid work indeed."[5]

Extracurricular rhetoric and persuasive writing were another matter. He helped organize the Liberal Debating Club, whose members held forth on crucial questions of the day. He competed in public-speaking contests. He joined the staff of the *Princeto-nian*, becoming editor his senior year. In the pages of the paper he expounded on all manner of subjects: the mode of selecting the captain of the baseball team, the excess of visible skin in the gymnasium, the woeful inattention to the persuasive arts in the curriculum of the college. "Why shall a thorough course in elocution not be the next acquisition to the College?" he demanded in one issue.[6] In another he instructed his readers on the aims and uses of oratory:

What is the object of oratory? Its object is persuasion and conviction—the control of other minds by a strange personal influence and power. What are the fields of labor open to us in our future life career as orators? The bar, the pulpit, the stump, the Senate chamber, the lecturer's platform.[7]

Public speaking and editorial writing led Wilson to politics. In the presidential campaign of 1876, he threw his support behind Samuel Tilden, the Democratic nominee. As a southerner, Wilson probably would have backed Tilden against any candidate the Republicans put forward, but Tilden's reputation as a reformer, in contrast to the spoilsmen who dominated the party of Grant, gave the New York governor a particular appeal. "Tomorrow the nation makes its choice between Samuel J. Tilden and R. B. Hayes," Wilson noted in his diary for November 6, 1876. "I most sincerely hope that it will be sensible enough to elect Tilden as I think the salvation of the country from frauds and the reviving of trade depends upon his election."[8] Yet with the sophistication of the college senior, Wilson refused to endorse the Democracy as a whole. "The Democrats will be very likely to abuse power if they get it," he predicted. "Men are greedy fellows as a rule."[9] (The 1876 election also marked the political coming-out of Harvard undergraduate Theodore Roosevelt, who paraded for Hayes.)

The balloting was agonizingly close. "Oh for some decision one way or the other in the election!" Wilson moaned as the votes were tallied.[10] When the results revealed that the voters had chosen Tilden but their electors Hayes, the outcome frustrated Wilson—as it did a great many Americans—and it piqued his curiosity as to whether this sort of thing happened in other countries. Looking to England, he became enamored of the great statesmen and orators of America's mother country. He copied the speeches of Edmund Burke into his commonplace book; he praised the elder William Pitt for a poetic imagination that "set his words fairly aglow with beauty."[11] John Bright's rhetoric revealed "the calmness of white heat."[12] William Gladstone's style was "a two-edged sword that can split fine hairs of distinction with no less precision than it can search out the heart of an opponent's plea, that can make the dexterous passes of dialectic fence with the same readiness with which it can cleave the defenses of prejudice."[13]

With admiration for British statesmen came enthusiasm for the political system that produced them. Wilson won a minor reputation with an essay published in the *International Review* shortly after his 1879 graduation, calling for measures to make the American cabinet responsible to Congress, as the British cabinet was responsible to the British Parliament. He adduced various arguments in support of his recommendation, starting with the negative evidence of ongoing corruption in the American system. But his central argument was that exposure to Congress, and to the debates that took place there, would cleanse the cabinet of the moral rot that infested the unexamined executive branch. At the same time, regular exchanges between those who crafted the laws and those who executed them would have a vivifying effect on the electorate, now discouraged because so often kept in the dark. "Debate is the essential function of a representative body," Wilson declared. "In the severe, distinct, and sharp enunciation of underlying principles, the unsparing examination and telling criticism of opposite positions, the careful, painstaking unraveling of all the issues involved, which are incident to the free discussion of questions of public policy, we see the best, the only effective means of educating public opinion."[14]

Not for decades would Wilson's contact with the world of politics be closer than secondhand, anything more intimate than the outside observations of the scholar. But these early assessments of the great statesmen certainly suggest a strong desire in the young Wilson to emulate those he admired. Gladstone, Bright, and the others won fame and influence by voicing the needs and desires of their countrymen. Throughout history, some men have gained power by the sword, others by the purse. Still others—the ones with whom Wilson identified—gained power by the compelling nature of their words.

In the editorial in which he had identified the vocations open to the orator, Wilson listed the bar first. Thus it was no leap for him to enroll in law school the autumn after his graduation from Princeton. He chose the University of Virginia, which, despite its reputation as the pride of the South, didn't impress him. "I can't say that my liking for life at the University increases as my acquaintance with it grows," he told one of his Princeton friends midway through his first year. "My judgment of the place is about this, that it is a splendid place for the education of the *mind*, but no sort of place for the education of the *man*."[15]

In fact, it was the law rather than the university that was the problem. The law, Wilson said, was "a hard task-master." And dull.

I wish now to record the confession that I am most terribly bored by the noble study of Law sometimes. . . . I think that it is the want of *variety* that disgusts me. Law served with some of the lighter and spicier sauces of literature would no doubt be at all times to us of the profession an exceedingly palatable dish. But when one has nothing but Law, served in all its dryness, set before him from one week's end to another, for month after month and for quarter after quarter, he tires of this uniformity of diet. This excellent thing, the Law, gets as monotonous as that other immortal article of food, Hash, when served with such endless frequency.[16]

Wilson stuck with law school for eighteen months. He would have quit earlier but for his father's admonition to persist. After its promising start, Dr. Wilson's career had bogged down, and he was feeling the midlife pinch of an unremunerative profession. He didn't want his son to suffer a like fate. The younger Wilson's answer was to plead ill health, which caused his mother to insist that he suspend his law studies and come home to recuperate. He did so in December of his second year (of a two-year curriculum) and never returned.

Living again with his parents was hardly the thing to excite a twenty-four-year-old. He grudgingly continued to study law on his own ("Stick to the law and its prospects," his father declared, "be they ever so depressing or disgusting")[17] even as he moonlighted in subjects more in keeping with his ambition and his conception of what counted in life. He read history and politics and practiced elocution. He took voice lessons, to strengthen and polish his delivery. "I make frequent extemporaneous addresses to the empty benches of my father's church in order to get a mastery of easy and correct and elegant expression, in preparation for the future," he told a Princeton friend. "My topics are most of them political, and I can sometimes almost see the benches smile at some of my opinions and deliverances."[18]

His familial claustrophobia peaked about the time he judged himself ready to try his luck as a lawyer. He moved to Atlanta in the spring of 1882 and became half of the firm Renick and Wilson. Business arrived slowly, not least since Wilson found the practice of law even more dismal than its study. "I am unfit for practice," he said after several months. "I have had just enough experience to prove that. In the first place, the atmosphere of the courts has proved very depressing to me. I cannot breathe freely nor smile readily in an atmosphere of broken promises, of wrecked estates, of neglected trusts, of unperformed duties, of crimes and of quarrels." He felt his soul shriveling and his heart hardening from constant exposure to the nether side of human nature. "But this is the least part of the argument," he continued. "Here lies the weight of it: my natural, and therefore predominant, tastes every day allure me from my law books; I throw away law reports for histories, and my mind runs after the solution of political, rather than of legal, problems, as if its keenest scent drew it after them by an unalterable instinct. My appetite is for general literature and my ambition is for writing."[19]

Far enough now from his father to ignore paternal remonstrance, Wilson elected to follow his instinct and ambition. A new graduate school had been established in Baltimore, endowed by the financial tycoon Johns Hopkins and modeled on the German universities that had served as finishing schools for ambitious American scholars. Wilson applied, was accepted, and in the autumn of 1883 enrolled.

At Hopkins he found a métier more congenial than law. He studied governments past and present and formulated his ideas into the book that served as his dissertation. *Congressional Government* (published in 1885) delineated the operation of what to Wilson was unarguably the most important branch of the federal government. Where his earlier essays had tended toward the prescriptive, this work stressed description. "I have abandoned the evangelical for the exegetical," he informed a friend.[20] Critics appreciated the distinction, praising both the book and its author. "The best critical writing on the American constitution which has appeared since the 'Federalist' papers," said one especially enthusiastic reviewer.[21]

The book launched Wilson's academic career. In 1885 he took a job at Bryn Mawr, where he taught the young ladies more than most of them wanted to know about the theory of government. (When reviewers had found fault with *Congressional Government*, they generally identified the author's emphasis on constitutional theory at the expense of legislative practice—an emphasis no doubt partly explained by the fact that Wilson never visited Congress before dissecting its operation.) From Bryn Mawr he transferred in 1888 to Connecticut's Wesleyan College, where he did the same to the men there. In 1890 his alma mater called him home, and he returned to Princeton.

. . .

Wilson's second coming to Princeton differed decidedly from his first. For one thing, he had a new name. Not long after graduation, and for reasons that remain unclear, he had dropped his first name, Thomas, in favor of his middle name, Woodrow. He told a close friend that in doing so he was honoring his mother's "special request."[22] Why she made this request, if in fact she did, after having apparently been satisfied with his use of Thomas for twenty-five years, he didn't say. Perhaps the request was of longer standing; if so, his reticence concealed his reason for acceding to it at this time. Old friends still called him Tommy, but to the rest of the world he was Woodrow.

For another thing, he was now a rising academic star and public thinker. His second book, *The State* (1889), cast the American system of government in comparative light, holding it up against its classical predecessors and its European contemporaries. It became a classroom standard and was translated into several foreign languages. Wilson meanwhile received and frequently accepted requests to contribute to popular journals and to lecture around the country on topics of historical and current interest.

Princeton greeted him enthusiastically. More than half the junior and senior classes signed up for his elective course in public law during his first semester. He didn't disappoint the young scholars and quickly gained a reputation as the best lecturer on campus. Upperclassmen raved about him to freshmen, who counted the semesters till they could take his courses.

His success at Princeton echoed around the university circuit. For several years he taught a short course at his other alma mater, Johns Hopkins. For a time he commuted weekly to New York to teach at the New York Law School. After two years at Princeton, the University of Illinois offered him its presidency.

The University of Virginia did the same—apparently willing to forgive his abrupt departure from the law school there.

But Princeton wouldn't let him get away. The trustees bumped up his salary till he was the highest-paid professor on campus. They adjusted his teaching schedule to suit his off-campus engagements. They gave him a leading role at the sesquicentennial of the college (at which it formally changed its name from the College of New Jersey and became a university). And in 1902 they voted unanimously to make him Princeton's president.

In those days of fewer universities and greater deference to authority, the presidency of a major university conferred uncommon stature on the incumbent. In Wilson's case, the office enhanced and ramified an already substantial reputation. Till now an expert on American and comparative politics, he became a spokesman for education and the molding of young America.

As it happened, the country was peculiarly attuned at this time to a marriage of politics and education. The first decade of the twentieth century witnessed the emergence on the national stage of progressivism, that congeries of reform which encompassed all manner of worthy causes, from conservation and corporate regulation to consumer protection and immigration restriction, from prohibition and workmen's compensation to women's suffrage and primary elections. What connected the sundry elements of this movement was an almost unquestioning faith in education as an instrument of democratic betterment. The education the progressives endorsed was broadly construed, starting in the schools but extending beyond the walls of the classroom. It included the exposés of the investigative journalists whom Theodore Roosevelt—the first progressive president, and the country's chief executive when Wilson took over at

Princeton—called "muckrakers." It included the reports of the myriad commissions appointed to examine this aspect or that of municipal corruption, statehouse shenanigans, and other forms of incest among corporate and political power brokers. And it included the lectures, articles, and books of those persons who headed the great educational institutions of the country, men such as Seth Low at Columbia, Charles Eliot at Harvard, and Woodrow Wilson at Princeton.

As Princeton president, Wilson met many of the most influential individuals in America. J. P. Morgan, Mark Twain, and Booker T. Washington attended his installation. Theodore Roosevelt had marked the date on his calendar, but a trolley car accident prevented his coming; the president made it up by attending an Army-Navy football game played at Princeton, and bringing along Secretary of State Elihu Root and much military brass. Andrew Carnegie dropped by the campus to make a donation. George Harvey, the editor of *Harper's Weekly*, which serialized Wilson's successful and influential *History of the American People* (published in book form in 1902), introduced the author around New York.

And yet, even as Wilson earned a national name, trouble developed at Princeton. Academic politics are known for their pettiness, and to outside observers, the most bitter fight of Wilson's presidency at Princeton did indeed seem small. The graduate dean, Andrew West, wanted to locate the graduate school some distance from the undergraduate college. He cited pedagogical reasons, but few observers doubted that beneath the rationale was his desire to maintain his independence from the rest of the university and from Wilson. Wilson had his own educational reasons for wanting the graduate school kept close to the college, but for him, too, the central issue was the independence of the graduate school, which Wilson wanted to limit. West was as clever as he was determined, and he lined up a donor to fund his freedom, thereby placing Wilson in the awkward position of looking a handsome gift horse in the mouth. The Wilson-West dispute split the alumni and the trustees. Eventually Wilson was forced to capitulate—although not to admit error. "The beauty about a Scotch-Irishman is that he not only thinks he is right, but knows he is right," he said, joking at himself but not at his judgment. "I have not departed from the faith of my ancestors."[23] West won his freedom, and Wilson began seeking an exit from Princeton.

He didn't have to look long. Since the Civil War, the Democratic party had wandered in the wilderness regarding the presidency, with Grover Cleveland being the sole exception to a half century of Republican chief executives. Of late the Democrats had been reduced to renominating William Jennings Bryan, who had been a stirring stump presence in 1896 but in 1900 and especially in 1908 simply seemed stale. The problem was partly the Democrats' lack of imagination but also the structure of national politics. The events surrounding the Civil War had made the South the stronghold of the Democrats, and while this was no handicap to the party in Congress—southern Democratic senators and congressmen held their own with Republicans from other sections—it hampered the party in presidential elections, in which candidates had to appeal to a national electorate. Tainted by secession and rebellion, the Democrats had difficulty fielding credible candidates.

After Bryan's 1908 defeat, certain Democratic strategists began searching for a new kind of candidate—one young enough to have missed the war, one with a national reputation, although not necessarily a reputation acquired in the practice of politics, and one with southern connections but not so closely identified with the South as to tempt the Republicans to wave the bloody shirt one more time. As Wilson's star rose above Princeton, and as his speeches and writings drew the approval of ever larger audiences, he seemed the answer to many Democratic prayers.

But was he interested? By all evidence, he considered the questions of American governance vital and compelling; but would he run for office? Editor George Harvey put the question directly: Would Wilson accept the nomination if it were offered? Without committing himself, Wilson responded that he would give the matter "very serious consideration."[24]

This was all Harvey needed to hear, and he began talking Wilson up among the Democratic leadership. The party bosses required convincing. The last thing they wanted was some professor telling them how to manage their affairs. Yet others in the party saw Wilson as the Democrats' return ticket from exile, as the one who could rescue the party from terminal Bryanism. They told the bosses that Wilson's very inexperience would render him that much more pliable when elected. He would have no choice but to heed the wisdom of the men who made practical politics their calling.

Because 1910 was not a presidential year, the pro-Wilson forces had an opportunity to test their man on a small stage. They proposed to nominate him for New Jersey governor. New Jersey's Democratic regulars, including boss James Smith, were still skeptical, so they sent a letter inquiring whether Wilson would disrupt the work they had done over many years. Wilson replied that he would not. "I would be perfectly willing to assure Mr. Smith that I would not, if elected Governor, set about 'fighting and breaking down the existing Democratic organization and replacing it with one of my own,'" he said. "The last thing I should think of would be building up a machine of my own."[25]

Wilson was duly nominated by the Democrats, whereupon he resigned the Princeton presidency. The campaign—for the governorship, but implicitly for the presidency—began with his acceptance address, in which he summoned his party to a higher politics. "Government is not a warfare of interests," he declared. "We shall not gain our ends by heat and bitterness, which makes it impossible to think either calmly or fairly. Government is a matter of common counsel, and everyone must come into the consultation with the purpose to yield to the general view, the view which seems most nearly to correspond with the common interests." Wilson sensed a new day in American politics. "We are witnessing a renaissance of public spirit, a reawakening of sober public opinion, a revival of the power of the people, the beginning of an age of thoughtful reconstruction that makes our thought hark back to the great age in which Democracy was set up in America." And in the name of democracy he and those who thought like him would march forward to victory. "Is not our own ancient party the party disciplined and made ready for this great task? Shall we not forget ourselves in making it the instrument of righteousness for the state and for the nation?"[26]

The delegates loved the speech. Wilson tried to keep it short, but they wouldn't let him stop. As the *Trenton True American* reported the next day, "The delegates were so deeply impressed by Dr. Wilson's oratory and were so desirous of hearing more of it that he was greeted with many cries of: 'Go on!' and 'You're all right!'" So he extemporaneously amplified his remarks, concluding several minutes later with a stirring peroration:

America is not distinguished so much by its wealth and material power as by the fact that it was born with an ideal, a purpose to serve mankind. And all mankind has sought her as a haven of equal justice. When I look upon the American flag before me, I think sometimes that it is made of parchment and blood. The white in it stands for parchment, the red in it signifies blood—parchment on which was written the rights of men, and blood that was spilled to make these rights real. Let us devote the Democratic party to the recovery of these rights.

The *True American* described the denouement: "At the conclusion of this masterly effort Dr. Wilson was mobbed by the delegates, and he had to be rescued by the police, who went to his aid and cleared a way to the stage door where an automobile was in waiting."[27]

Progressives in New Jersey thrilled to this new voice, even as reformers across the country eavesdropped excitedly. In certain respects, Wilson made a stronger national candidate than a state candidate. National progressives could revel in his rhetoric about democratic responsibility, while the local ward heelers had to wonder what they would do if the professor were elected. They wondered the more as the campaign continued, for, with the nomination safely in hand, Wilson—acting partly on instinct, it would seem, and partly on what he had learned from a career studying politics—distanced himself from the Democratic regulars as the election approached. The result was a resounding victory. In a heavy turnout, Wilson bested his Republican rival by nearly two to one.

Hardly had the votes been counted when Wilson's backers began looking to 1912. The New Jersey bosses required only slightly longer to do the same. Wilson's first order of gubernatorial business was to engineer the overthrow of boss Smith, whose support had been crucial in Wilson's nomination but who symbolized the old style of politics Wilson had pledged to eliminate. Not unnaturally, Smith accounted Wilson an ungrateful wretch and asserted that the governor's double cross was "striking evidence of his aptitude in the art of foul play."[28] Another member of the old guard, Democratic party chairman James Nugent, likewise got the boot and likewise felt misused; he called Wilson "an ingrate and a liar."[29] Those regulars who clung to power reckoned that their survival might well depend on promoting Wilson to Washington.

The object of their anger affected uninterest in higher office but nonetheless launched an informal presidential campaign. A cross-country speaking tour had nothing to do with the governance of New Jersey and everything to do with getting Wilson before the voters. In the South he was a Virginian; in the North and West he was a Jerseyman. Everywhere he was a stirring speaker, a teacher taking his lectures to the people. With practice his message sharpened; the lines that elicited the loudest applause were those that cast the struggle for reform in terms of the people against the interests. At first George Harvey and *Harper's* hailed the hard-charging governor, but eventually Wilson's attacks on corporate wrongdoing frightened even Harvey.

But by then the Wilson juggernaut had become nearly unstoppable. The election of 1912 was the first in which party primaries played an important role. On the Republican side, they prompted Theodore Roosevelt, who won most of the GOP primaries but lost the nomination to incumbent William Howard Taft, to bolt the Republicans and run as the candidate of the Progressive, or Bull Moose, party. The Democrats had no incumbent, and although the party regulars favored House Speaker Champ Clark of Missouri at the national convention in Baltimore, the Democrats' two-thirds requirement for nomination enabled Wilson to fend off Clark while seeking allies beyond the ranks of recognized progressives. For ballot after ballot Clark and the regulars hammered Wilson and the upstarts; for ballot after ballot the progressives patiently enlisted reinforcements. The break came when William Jennings Bryan, judging the professor preferable to the politico, swung to Wilson. With Bryan's backing, Wilson passed Clark on the thirtieth ballot and garnered the winning two-thirds on the forty-sixth.

The general campaign of 1912 was one of the great contests of American political history. Roosevelt's rhetorical energy was a known fact of political life, and although he no longer commanded the bully pulpit (a phrase that, like "muckrakers," "malefactors of great wealth," and "the big stick," he had already added to the American lexicon), he took the stump with customary verve. Roosevelt injected a further element of drama into the contest when, after an attempted assassination late in the campaign, he nonetheless mounted the dais and gave an impassioned speech even as his own blood stained his shirt a gaudy crimson.

Wilson couldn't compete with Roosevelt on the Rough Rider's terms and knew not to try. Wilson's approach was cooler and more cerebral yet inspired by a passion of his own. The compelling question of the day, he said, was what to do about the trusts, the corporate combines that had squeezed the life out of business competition and were extorting excessive profits from the American people. Roosevelt also assailed the trusts, but where Roosevelt wanted to rein in the trusts by regulating them, Wilson demanded their destruction—their breakup into parts that would have to compete for customers' favor rather than dictate the terms on which they would deign to deal with customers. "The center of all our economic difficulties is that there is not freedom of enterprise in the United States," Wilson told a Detroit audience. For a generation the captains of industry and finance had conspired to strangle competition—which was to say, to strangle those enterprises that had long been the hope of the hard working and the promise of the American future. "The inventive genius and initiative of the American people is being held back by the fact that our industrial field is so controlled that new entries, newcomers, new adventurers, independent men, are feared, and if they will not go partners in the game with those already in the control of it, they will be excluded." The business of the American government was not to accept the trusts as inevitable, as Roosevelt proposed, but to render them impotent by restoring real competition. "What I am interested in is laws that will give the little man a start, that will give him a chance to show these fellows that he has brains enough to compete with them and can presently make his local market a national market and his national market a world market, and put them to their mettle to do the business more intelligently and economically and systematically than he can."[30]

As the campaign continued, Wilson returned again and again to this idea that the country must restore individual liberty, now threatened as it hadn't been threatened since the American Revolution.

Here at the turning of the ways, when we are at last asking ourselves, "Can we get a free government that will serve us, and when we get it, will it set us free?" they say, "No, you can't have a free government, and you ought not to desire to be set free. We know your interests. We will obtain everything that you need by beneficent regulation. It isn't necessary to set you free. It is only necessary to take care of you." Ah, that way lies the path of tyranny; that way lies the destruction of independent, free institutions.[31]

His opponent—Wilson leveled all his fire at Roosevelt, ignoring Taft—was determined to foist a new, twisted vision on the American people, Wilson said. He himself would stick with the traditional verities.

The vision of America will never change. America once, when she was a little people, sat upon a hill of vantage and had a vision of the future. She saw men happy because they were free. She saw them free because they were equal. She saw them banded together because they had the spirit of brothers. She saw them safe because they did not wish to impose upon one another. And that vision is not changed. . . . America will move forward, if she moves forward at all, only with her face set to that same sun of promise. Just so soon as she forgets the sun in the heavens, just so soon as she looks so intently upon the road before her and around her that she does not know where it leads, then will she forget what America was created for, and her light will go out, and the nations will grope again in darkness, and they will say, "Where are those who prophesied a day of freedom for us? Where are the lights that we followed? Where is the torch that the runners bore? Where are those who bade us hope? Where came in those whispers of dull despair?"[32]

Listeners responded to Wilson in a way he could only have dreamed of earlier, when he spoke to those imaginary audiences in his father's empty church. A crowd at Madison Square Garden shouted and stamped for an hour *before* he spoke. ("It was a wonderful demonstration," Wilson acknowledged, but it had a drawback. "The thing completely rattled me and I forgot my speech. I didn't deliver the speech I had thought out so carefully.")[33] Roosevelt had borrowed a slogan for his own program: the "New Nationalism." Wilson riposted with an emphasis on the individual: the "New Freedom."

Americans preferred Wilson's formula, or at any rate they gave its author a plurality of their votes: 6.3 million for Wilson, to 4.1 million for Roosevelt and 3.5 million for Taft. The electoral college, functioning as it was designed to do, converted Wilson's plurality into an electoral majority: 435 for Wilson against 88 for Roosevelt and 8 for Taft.

The circumstances of Wilson's election presented him with a peculiar set of challenges. Having won but a minority of the popular vote, he could hardly claim a personal mandate. Yet he and the other reform candidate, Roosevelt, had polled an overwhelming majority together, indicating that Americans solidly supported new reins on big business, even if they differed on the brand of the bridle and length of the halter.

Wilson's relationship with his own party was likewise problematic. "There has been a change of government," he said in his inaugural address. "It began two years ago, when the House of Representatives became Democratic by a decisive majority. It has now been completed."[34] And so it had, with the Democrats adding control of the Senate and the presidency to their conquest of the House. But as Wilson's observation suggested, he wasn't the herald of change so much as its beneficiary. He liked to think, and had argued, that with a standpat candidate like Champ Clark, the Democrats would have gone down to defeat. And he was probably right. Yet the split in the Republican party had as much to do with Wilson's victory as his own personal appeal. On March 4, 1913, the Democrats were happy to link arms in helping their new man move into the White House; but on March 5, those at the other end of Pennsylvania Avenue, including Clark, began reminding him that he wasn't the only Democrat in town, and perhaps not even the most powerful.

The nature of the campaign Wilson had run didn't help matters. All successful reform candidates confront a dilemma on entering office. Having promised to turn the rascals out, they have no choice but to make a start on the evictions. But no one wins major office, and certainly not the presidency, without help from the powers-that-be. Those powers expect compensation, and if they don't receive it they can paralyze the new man.

Wilson struck a balance between reform and retention, a balance that dissatisfied—as such balances do—both the true believers among his partisans and the hard core of the holdovers. Wilson set the tone for what followed in a postelection huddle with William McCombs, the head of the Democratic national committee, who came to remind Wilson of the role of the party organization in his victory.[35] "Before we proceed," Wilson declared, according to McCombs's recollection, "I wish it clearly understood that I owe you nothing."

"I modestly suggested that I might be given credit for doing a little toward his nomination and election," McCombs recalled.

"Whether you did little or much," Wilson answered, in what McCombs characterized as a haughty tone of voice, "remember that God *ordained that I should be the next president of the United States.* Neither you nor any other mortal or mortals could have prevented that."

Whether Wilson said these precise words is difficult to know; McCombs, as one of the ousted, had an ax to grind. But the quoted passage almost certainly captured Wilson's general feelings on the subject, and the episode revealed something fundamental about the man who became the twenty-eighth president of the United States. Though Wilson had chosen a different career from his father, he was as orthodox a Presbyterian as the Reverend Wilson. From youth he had read the Bible daily and attended religious services faithfully; he still did so. During those periods of his life when he kept a diary, he commonly closed with "Thank God for health and strength."[36] He had been taught that nothing in the world happened without divine participation, and nothing in his experience of the world had caused him to question that conclusion. Because he typically believed that he acted according to God's plan, he could evince a certitude his rivals found infuriating. They grew even more infuriated when he suddenly changed course, as he could do when a tactical reversal didn't trespass on what he considered underlying principle. Mere mortals wrestled with doubt and confusion, but the self-assured Wilson possessed, to judge by his manner, a direct line to heaven. He wouldn't have put it quite that way, but he did think God was usually on his side, and the alliance afforded him a moral serenity few could match.

Though Wilson might brush off McCombs, there was one representative of the party who had to be recognized. William Jennings Bryan's support at Baltimore had been crucial in winning Wilson the nomination; moreover, despite Bryan's three losses in presidential elections, the Great Commoner still exercised a powerful hold on rural rank-and-file Democrats. His continued support would be essential if Wilson wished to stamp his own imprint on the party's program. For years Bryan had taken an active, if idiosyncratic, interest in foreign affairs, opposing imperialism and war and advocating arbitration of international disputes. Many in both parties considered him a lamb among wolves on matters diplomatic. But because Wilson didn't think foreign affairs would play an important role in his administration, and because what little he knew about the world at large inclined him to hope that Bryan's biblically inspired pacifism could become a blueprint for international relations, he gave the Nebraskan the premier cabinet appointment, as secretary of state.

Other appointments rewarded other constituencies. William McAdoo, a party wheelhorse from New York, became secretary of the treasury. Josephus Daniels, a North Carolina editor who had handled Democratic publicity during the campaign, was named secretary of the navy—a post that proved unexpectedly important before long. (Daniels's assistant at the Navy Department was an athletic young man with a familiar last name: Franklin D. Roosevelt, the former president's fifth cousin and nephew-by-marriage.) Conservative Texan Albert Sidney Burleson was selected for postmaster general.

From the start, however, it was apparent that this administration would be run from the White House. As his row with Andrew West at Princeton suggested, Wilson wasn't much for delegation. He liked to keep the levers of power close. Besides, as a political newcomer and an avowed outsider, he had few friends or associates with the requisite qualifications for cabinet office. The men he appointed were all strangers to him. Perhaps he would learn to trust their counsel and judgment, but not easily or soon.

Yet every president needs advice, and for this Wilson turned to two men he didn't initially appoint to office. One was Louis Brandeis, a crusading Boston lawyer and author who inspired a whole generation of progressive reformers, including Wilson. Politically, Brandeis was too hot for a new administration to handle; mere rumors that he might head the Justice Department and direct antitrust prosecution sent Wall Street's blood pressure up and its share prices down. Wilson wasn't worried about the cardiac health of the boardrooms, but he didn't want to start his presidency with a financial panic, and he contented himself with making Brandeis an unofficial adviser.

Closer than Brandeis was Edward House. A wealthy Texan who appreciated the honorary title "colonel" bestowed by a grateful governor of the Lone Star state, House possessed a kind of ambition more common in Europe than America. He realized that he lacked the gifts required for election in his own right, so he aimed to be the Richelieu to someone else's Louis. House grew aware of Wilson as the latter's star was rising over the Delaware River, and he set about ingratiating himself to the New Jersey governor. The strategy succeeded brilliantly. "You are the only person in the world with whom I can discuss everything," Wilson wrote in 1915. "There are some I can tell one thing and others another, but you are the only one to whom I can make an entire clearance of mind."[37] Wilson explained to a mutual acquaintance, "Mr. House is my second personality. He is my independent self. His thoughts and mine are one."[38] On another occasion Wilson declared to House, "I would rather have your judgment than that of anybody I know."[39]

Most observers wondered at this sudden intimacy. Surely, they surmised, the president must know that House was using him. House privately admitted that he was. "My physical handicaps"—his visage was sometimes compared to a rodent's—"and my temperament make it necessary for me to work through other men. I was like a disembodied spirit seeking a corporeal form. I found my opportunity in Woodrow Wilson."[40]

Wilson's attachment to House is harder to explain. Part of it was political—or antipolitical. At a time when nearly everyone Wilson encountered wanted a favor or a job, House sought only the opportunity to give advice. Wilson had a sufficiently robust sense of himself to believe that he wouldn't be corrupted by mere advice. The other part of the Wilson-House equation was personal. Wilson had few friends, and House certainly *acted* friendly. He was personable, intelligent, and discreet—a combination that would have appealed to any president, but especially one as nongregarious as Wilson.

The third of Wilson's intimates was Joseph Tumulty, his private secretary. In those days before the metastasizing of the executive bureaucracy, Tumulty served simultaneously as chief of staff, director of communications, national security adviser, and counsel to the president. Irish by ancestry, New Jerseyite by birth, Democratic by decision, progressive by preference, Tumulty linked up with Wilson during the campaign for governor. He impressed the candidate, who rewarded his service with appointment as secretary and political adviser. When Wilson went to Washington, Tumulty joined him. Some observers puzzled at the partnership between the Presbyterian professor and the Catholic pol; especially in the South, where Rome rivaled Africa as the bête noire of the reviving Ku Klux Klan, Tumulty cost Wilson support. But Tumulty was efficient, firm with intruders on Wilson's time, ruthless with tamperers against the president's prerogatives, and sensitive to his superior's needs and desires. No one served Wilson longer or more faithfully.

Elected on a pledge to free the American people from thrall to the trusts, Wilson at once set about redeeming his pledge. And he did so in a manner that, while natural to him, marked a minor revolution in American politics.

The Constitution specifies that the president shall from time to time report to Congress on the state of the Union and recommend legislation. George Washington and John Adams interpreted this charge literally and delivered their messages in person. Thomas Jefferson abandoned the practice as smacking of royal speeches from the throne. For the next century presidential messages to Congress were read by a clerk, nearly always without the energy and conviction their executive authors would have given them.

Wilson, enamored of oratory and confident of his persuasive abilities, decided to resurrect the eighteenth-century tradition. Shortly after the inauguration, Tumulty revealed that the president would be going to the Capitol in person to address the legislature. This break from long practice created a stir in itself, as Wilson intended. Critics aware of his admiration for British forms of government accused him of Anglophilia and perhaps megalomania. "I regret all this cheap and tawdry imitation of English royalty," said John Williams, Democratic senator from Mississippi.[41]

Wilson ignored the carping. "I think that this is the only dignified way for the President to address the houses on the opening of a session, instead of sending the thing up by messenger and letting the clerk read it perfunctorily in the familiar clerk's tone of voice," he said.[42] When Wilson got to Capitol Hill, he told the combined gathering of senators and representatives, "I am very glad indeed to have this opportunity to address the two Houses directly and to verify for myself the impression that the President of the United States is a person, not a mere department of the Government hailing Congress from some isolated island of jealous power, sending messages, not speaking naturally and with his own voice—that he is a human being trying to cooperate with other human beings in a common service. After this pleasant experience I shall feel quite normal in all our dealings with one another."[43]

Not everyone in Congress found the experience pleasant. The House and especially the Senate had their own traditions, and the currently controlling Democratic leaders, including Clark, had their own plans. But they could hardly deny the president the opportunity to speak, as he well understood.

On this first visit Wilson let his mere presence make his point: that he intended to be no island of executive power, separate from the lawmaking authority of Congress. He had long advocated a closer link between the executive and the legislature; now that he headed the executive, he would become that link himself, leading Congress by his presence and by the power of his words. Again and again during the eight years of his presidency, Wilson rode from the White House up Capitol Hill to address the lawmakers under their own roof. In doing so he captured their attention—and the attention of the country, which was intrigued by the sight of the president instructing Congress on what the welfare of the nation required. This innovation—or rather this return to long-abandoned practice—was one of the hallmarks of the Wilson presidency, and one of his lasting contributions to American governance. Ever since Wilson, a president's ability to take his message to Congress, and through Congress to the American people, has been one of his most potent tools; and the occasions on which presidents have addressed joint sessions have included some of the most memorable in American history.

The purpose of Wilson's first visit—besides unveiling a new style of executive leadership—was to announce a plan to revise the nation's tax structure. From the late eighteenth century to the early twentieth, the most important federal taxes were excise taxes and import taxes. The former were intermittently controversial, sparking, for example, the Whiskey Rebellion of 1794, which caused George Washington to saddle up once more and lead federal troops against the rural Pennsylvania insurgents. Import taxes, or tariffs, were less visible to ordinary men and women, and therefore less likely to elicit violence, but they were for that reason more susceptible to pressure from lobbyists. The tariff advocates preached protection of domestic producers against predatory foreigners. This argument, which held a certain amount of water during America's national and economic infancy, was leaking badly as the country became an industrial behemoth. But the protected producers stubbornly defended their preferences, which afforded them a profit premium at the expense of foreign producers and of consumers who had to pay the toll.

Yet the tariff was more than a guarantee of profits. Progressives like Wilson often argued that "the tariff made the trusts." Their point was that the tariff sheltered big business from competition and encouraged the growth of monopolies. The tariff simultaneously fostered political corruption, as the monopolies sought to preserve their protected position. Import taxes were worth many millions to favored firms, which contributed regularly and heavily to the legislators responsible for writing the tariff laws. In taking on the tariff, Wilson struck a blow at once for consumers and for good government.

Wilson announced his position in his maiden speech to Congress. "We must abolish everything that bears even the semblance of privilege or of any kind of artificial advantage," he declared, "and put our business men and producers under the stimulation of a constant necessity to be efficient, economical, and enterprising, masters of competitive supremacy, better workers and merchants than any in the world. . . . The object of the tariff duties henceforth laid must be effective competition, the whetting of American wits by contest with the wits of the rest of the world."[44]

From the House chamber that day Wilson retired to the President's Room of the Capitol, where he caucused with the Democratic senators for more than an hour. His style behind closed doors was more personal yet no less persuasive than in public forums. "We always come away feeling that we have been convinced not by Mr. Wilson, certainly not driven or bossed by him," one Democratic lawmaker explained, "but with the feeling that we are all—President, Congress and people—in the presence of an irresistible situation. Here are the facts, he says; here are the principles; here are our obligations as Democrats. What are we going to do about it? He has a curious way of making one feel that he, along with all of us, is perfectly helpless before the facts in the case."[45]

Wilson maintained the pressure for tariff reform during the spring of 1913. After Oscar Underwood of Alabama, the Democratic chairman of the House Ways and Means Committee and a strong Wilson ally on tariff reform, introduced a measure sharply reducing rates on a wide array of imports, the tariff lobbyists counterattacked. The protection gang defended every ingot of steel, bolt of cloth, pair of shoes, sack of sugar, and bale of cotton as though the survival of the republic hung in the balance. Against the lobby, and over the heads of the lawmakers, Wilson took his case to the people.

I think that the public ought to know the extraordinary exertions being made by the lobby in Washington to gain recognition for certain alterations of the tariff bill. Washington has seldom seen so numerous, so industrious, or so insidious a lobby. The newspapers are being filled with paid advertisements calculated to mislead the judgment of public men not only, but also the public opinion of the country itself. There is every evidence that money without limit is being spent to sustain this lobby, and to create an appearance of a pressure of public opinion antagonistic to some of the chief items of the tariff bill.[46]

It was a risky maneuver: to claim that those who differed with him were paid agents of the pro-tariff forces. Some editors called him on it, complaining that he was trying to stifle free debate. But who could say for certain that the complainers weren't part of the conspiracy? Conspiracy or not, Wilson summoned sufficient support to extract a landmark tariff reduction from Congress, the first in more than a generation. It was a great victory for the new president, and recognized as such by friends and foes alike.

As matters happened, however, a rider to the tariff bill had a larger impact than the tariff reductions themselves. The new tariff had hardly taken effect before the world war deranged

Atlantic shipping and obviated much of the revised schedule. But the rate reducers, acting under the recently ratified Sixteenth Amendment, had included a provision instituting an income tax, designed to replace revenues lost to the tariff trimming. The income tax rates were very modest at first, starting at 1 percent on incomes over $4,000 and rising to 2 percent on incomes over $20,000. Yet they incorporated the progressive principle of increasing with income, and this, combined with the reduction of reliance on tariffs, which, as consumption taxes, tended to be regressive, shifted the burden of supporting the government from the worse off to the better.

No trust loomed larger in the progressive mind than the "money trust," which was essentially impervious to tariff reform. To tackle the money trust—the interlocking directorate of investors and bankers that controlled the allotment of capital among America's major enterprises—Wilson adopted a different strategy. Ever since Andrew Jackson had killed the second Bank of the United States in the mid-1830s, the country had been without a central bank. Hundreds of private banks furnished the financial needs of the nation's burgeoning economy, but furnished them badly, by the evidence of the financial panics and depressions that recurrently prostrated the economy and seared the national consciousness. No central authority controlled the nation's money supply or coordinated the actions of the private banks. In good times, this laissez-faire approach didn't do much damage, but when something jolted business confidence, the tremor often rumbled through the entire system, wreaking havoc from coast to coast.

Nearly everyone agreed that something had to be done. The money men themselves wanted a central bank under private ownership and control but with government's blessing to issue currency and otherwise direct the economy. William Jennings Bryan, who had cut his populist teeth campaigning against the big bankers, denounced this idea as giving the money men more power than they already had. Bryan and his farm-state supporters demanded that the banking system come under federal control.

If Wilson had known more about banking, he might have taken an early lead on the issue. But his knowledge of economics was thin and academic, and his grasp of practical finance even sparer. So he called in Louis Brandeis for a crash course in banking and money. Brandeis urged the president to hold out against the bankers. Participation in the new system might include private banks, Brandeis said, but ultimate control, especially over the money supply, must rest with the government. Wilson agreed.

The fight over the banking bill filled the summer of 1913. Wilson returned to the Capitol, where he told a sweaty session of Congress that the national welfare demanded action on the money front. "The control of the system of banking and of issue which our new laws are to set up must be public, not private, must be vested in the Government itself, so that the banks may be the instruments, not the masters, of business and of individual enterprise and initiative."[47]

This formula—of banks as the instrument of individual enterprise, not its master—became the touchstone for Wilson and the reformers during the months that followed. The bankers and their legislative allies threw one hurdle after another in front of the president's plan, calling it socialistic, proposing spurious amendments, obfuscating and delaying when defeat became inevitable. But finally Wilson won. Two days before Christmas he signed the Federal Reserve Act, which left ownership of the banks in private hands but vested oversight in a board appointed by the president. Although Wilson's founding compromise was inspired by the political pressures of the moment, during the next ninety years it came to seem inspired by higher forces. The Federal Reserve system stumbled badly after the stock market crash of 1929, but with some tinkering it regained its feet and proceeded to manage the American economy remarkably well for the rest of the century.

The third prong of Wilson's attack on the trusts—the third part of the New Freedom in action—was revision of antitrust law. The Sherman Act of 1890 had provided the basis for antitrust prosecutions initiated by the Roosevelt and Taft administrations, but despite some signal victories, including the 1911 breakup of John D. Rockefeller's Standard Oil Company, the Sherman law allowed lesser or more artful monopolists to go free. Wilson determined to close the loopholes, and before Congress had caught its breath after the fight for the Federal Reserve, he was back on Capitol Hill, telling the legislature why the country needed stronger antitrust legislation and how the muscling-up might proceed. Shortly thereafter Henry Clayton of Alabama, the Democratic chairman of the House Judiciary Committee, introduced a bill embodying Wilson's recommendations. The Clayton bill specified various trade practices as illegally unfair, and, in a move designed to get the attention of the boardrooms, it authorized criminal penalties, including jail time, for directors of firms found in violation.

The bill got the intended attention, and business groups fought bitterly against it. So did other groups, for opposite reasons. Some progressives with experience in antitrust law predicted that an attempt to define unfair trade practices in statute would fail. Anything too narrow would be evaded by clever corporate attorneys; anything too broad would be rejected by the courts. Better, these reformers argued, to establish a federal trade commission empowered to determine, instance by instance and industry by industry, what constituted unfair practice.

Wilson at first opposed the idea of a commission, which was what Roosevelt had advocated in the 1912 campaign and Wilson had rejected. He didn't think corporate attorneys were that much cleverer than the government's counsel. "Surely we are sufficiently familiar with the actual processes and methods of monopoly and of the many hurtful restraints of trade to make definition possible, at any rate up to the limits of what experience has disclosed," he asserted. "These practices, being now abundantly disclosed, can be explicitly and item by item forbidden by statute."[48]

Yet the more he learned about the intricacies of antitrust law, the more he tilted toward giving the commission idea a chance. And when the economy slipped into recession in late 1913, he discovered additional merit in the commission approach. Business leaders were blaming him for the recession, citing the scare he had given business by his tariff and banking measures. Wilson denied responsibility but recognized that a serious downturn would damage the Democrats in the 1914 elections and perhaps himself two years later. Business distrusted him already; if utterly alienated, it might sabotage him even to its own detriment.

Consequently, when important business groups indicated a preference for the commission scheme over the more rigid Clayton bill, Wilson backed the former. Some of the business lobbyists expected to capture the commission, as commissions had been captured in the past (and would be in the future). Others, less confident, simply liked the idea of working with regulators who could say in advance whether a proposed merger was legal or not, as opposed to dealing with prosecutors and judges who withheld their opinions until after the fact. Wilson found this latter argument persuasive, and when Brandeis gave the commission idea his approval, the president was convinced. The substitute measure, which created the Federal Trade Commission, passed Congress and in September 1914 received the president's signature. A somewhat weakened but still substantial Clayton bill likewise became law.

Surveying his handiwork in time for the 1914 congressional elections, Wilson pronounced it good. "Private control had shown its sinister face on every hand in America, had shown it for a long time, and sometimes very brazenly, in the trusts and in a virtual domination of credit by small groups of men," he said. The favorite hideout of this cabal had been the tariff, but the new tariff law forced the conspirators into the open. "The reduction of the tariff, the simplification of its schedules so as to cut away the jungle in which secret agencies had so long lurked, the correction of its inequalities . . . were an indispensable first step to reestablishing competition." The banking act had similar aims and was achieving similar success. "We have created a democracy of credit such as has never existed in this country before. . . . No group of bankers anywhere can get control; no one part of the country can concentrate the advantages and conveniences of the system upon itself for its own selfish advantage." As for the new antimonopoly measures, they closed a crucial gap in antitrust law. "Before these bills were passed, the law was already clear enough that monopolies once formed were illegal and could be dissolved by direct process of law. . . .

But there was no law to check the process by which monopoly was built up until the tree was full grown and its fruit developed, or, at any rate, until the full opportunity for monopoly had been created. With this new legislation there is clear and sufficient law to check and destroy the noxious growth in its infancy."[49]

# 2

---

# The Irony of Fate

At the time Wilson entered the White House, expertise in international affairs had never been a prerequisite for elective office in America. Only sporadically during the late eighteenth and nineteenth centuries did the world at large impinge importantly on the United States, and voters saw little reason to quiz candidates regarding their knowledge of and intentions toward that larger world. The Spanish-American War of 1898 gave Americans a greater stake in global affairs by planting Old Glory in the Philippines, and the start of construction on the Panama Canal a few years later heightened American sensitivity to what transpired en route to the isthmus. But otherwise most Americans continued to ignore the world, and in the 1912 election international affairs played almost no part.

This was lucky for Wilson, who was about as innocent on the subject as a man could be and still consider himself educated. He had traveled only a little, and only as a tourist. His foreign language skills were better than most of his compatriots' but didn't extend much beyond the reading knowledge required of history graduate students and, in Wilson's case, were soon lost by atrophy. In the rare instances when his research had required facility in languages other than English, he hired it. The simple fact of the matter was that Wilson had almost no interest in foreign countries and the people who lived there. To the degree he thought about foreigners, he assumed they were rather like Americans, if harder to comprehend. They lived under the same Heaven and served the same God, or ought to. Wilson understood his limitations. "It would be the irony of fate if my administration had to deal chiefly with foreign affairs," he told a friend just before inauguration.[1]

The irony set in at once. For years Mexico had been restive under the dictatorship of Porfirio Díaz, whose iron hand was growing arthritic with age. In 1911 a faction following Francisco Madero tossed Díaz out—to Europe, where he shortly died. But dismantling the old regime was more difficult than erecting a new one, and Madero was pushed aside, fatally, by the forces of Victoriano Huerta, whom Madero had enlisted to suppress the holdovers from the Díaz regime. Huerta thereupon arranged his own election as provisional president of Mexico and invited recognition from the United States and other powers.

It was at this point that Wilson entered the White House. The U.S. government and Americans with business interests and property in Mexico had long since made their peace with the Díaz regime; unsurprisingly, the groups that had supported Madero registered a certain lack of sympathy toward the yanquis. What the attitude of Huerta would be was left for Wilson to discover.

And perhaps to help determine. American financiers and property holders lobbied for recognition of Huerta, on grounds that Huerta could protect them against the revolutionary forces that had begun to emerge as Díaz was displaced. The professionals in the State Department suggested that precedent likewise pointed to recognition, in that America's historic practice was to inquire not how governments came into power but simply whether they controlled their country's territory and agreed to honor international obligations.

As a progressive, Wilson was unpersuaded by the pleas of the bankers. As a foreign-policy novice, he was unmoved by the lessons of the diplomats. As a moralist, he was offended by Huerta's double cross and complicity in the murder of Madero. As a student of governmental theory, he was suspicious of the irregularity of Huerta's election.

Wilson's misgivings summed to a decision against recognition. "We hold, as I am sure all thoughtful leaders of republican government everywhere hold, that just government rests always upon the consent of the governed, and that there can be no freedom without order based upon law and upon the public conscience and approval," he explained. "We shall look to make these principles the basis of mutual intercourse, respect, and helpfulness between our sister republics and ourselves." Speaking more directly of—and to—Huerta, the president continued, "We can have no sympathy with those who seek to seize the power of government to advance their own personal ends or ambition. We are the friends of peace, but we know that there can be no lasting or stable peace in such circumstances. As friends, therefore, we shall prefer those who act in the interest of peace and honor, who protect private rights and respect the restraints of constitutional provision."[2]

Wilson's preference for constitutional provisions turned into a litmus test for recognition of a Mexican government. The historical fact that constitutionalism had never been a significant feature of life in Mexico didn't bother him, nor the political likelihood that the present period of turbulence might not be the most propitious time for planting it there. Wilson's critics noted this, besides remarking that if his rule about disqualifying candidates who entered politics for personal ends or ambition were applied north of the border, the field of American aspirants to office would be substantially narrowed. Wilson couldn't dispute this conclusion, but he took it as evidence that American progressives had work to do.

The policy of nonrecognition turned out to be easier to proclaim than to practice. Suspicious of the State Department bureaucracy, and especially of the vehemently pro-Huerta American ambassador, Henry Lane Wilson, Wilson sent his own man to Mexico to assess the situation there. The reports William Bayard Hale wrote home cast Huerta in a harsh but not dismissive light. "General Huerta is an ape-like old man, of almost pure Indian blood. He may almost be said to subsist on alcohol. Drunk or only half-drunk (he is never sober), he never loses a certain shrewdness. He has been life-long a soldier, and one of the best in Mexico, and he knows no methods but those of force." Although his troops were hardly models of martial devotion—consisting of "captured rebels, released jail-birds and impressed peons"—Huerta was tough and wouldn't be dislodged easily. "He is a hard fighter, glories in the exercise of power, and I see no signs that he will abandon his office, except, as is possible, to take the field for a few months, so as to render himself legally eligible to take the presidency again under the pretence of election."[3]

Yet Huerta had enemies, and not just in Washington. A group of Madero's erstwhile supporters, calling themselves Constitutionalists and following the lead of Venustiano Carranza, raised the banner of anti-Huerta rebellion in northern Mexico. In the south and southeast, Emiliano Zapata was organizing the chronic rural unrest into a separate revolutionary force.

The hope of Wilson's nonrecognition policy was that the Mexicans would put their own house in order, with the United States promising recognition for successful straightening up. But the house grew only more disorderly with each passing month, and Wilson was compelled to consider stronger action. American property- and bond-holders clamored for protection; more worryingly, foreign governments were threatening to intervene. Wilson knew enough about American foreign policy to understand that since 1823, when James Monroe had enunciated his eponymous doctrine, a cardinal principle of American policy had been to limit the influence of foreign powers (other than the United States, that is) in Latin America. Theodore Roosevelt had added a corollary to the Monroe Doctrine, declaring that in the event Latin American countries reneged on international commitments or otherwise behaved badly, the United States would chastise them, lest the Europeans be tempted to do so. Wilson had often thought Roosevelt a bully in international affairs, but as he now observed the anarchy in Mexico and contemplated British or German marines occupying Mexico's ports, he couldn't deny this branch of Big Stick logic.

Again avoiding the State Department, Wilson sent another special emissary south. John Lind knew as little about Mexico as Wilson did, but his heart was in the rightly progressive place, and as Wilson's man he could speak in Wilson's voice. "The Government of the United States does not feel at liberty any longer to stand inactively by while it becomes daily more evident that no real progress is being made towards the establishment of a government at the City of Mexico which the country will obey and respect," Wilson said, through Lind. Under such circumstances, Washington deemed itself obliged to offer counsel— "not only because of our genuine desire to play the part of a friend, but also because we are expected by the powers of the world to act as Mexico's nearest friend." Declaring that "all America cries out for a settlement" of the Mexican conflict, Wilson specified four conditions that would make a settlement satisfactory to Washington: a cease-fire among all parties, free elections, Huerta's disqualification from candidacy, and agreement by all parties to honor the election results. Should the conditions be met, the United States would recognize the government chosen.[4]

Not surprisingly, Huerta rejected Wilson's offer, even after Lind sweetened it with the promise of a large American loan to the Huerta regime should he agree to hold elections and not be a candidate. Huerta denounced this transparent bribe and vowed never to sell his country's honor for a mess of gringo pottage.

Wilson was disappointed but not surprised. "Our friend Huerta is a diverting brute!" he told an old friend. "He is always so perfectly in character: so false, so sly, so full of bravado (the bravado of ignorance, chiefly), and yet so courageous, too, and determined—such a mixture of weak and strong, of ridiculous and respectable! One moment you long for his blood, out of mere justice for what he has done, and the next you find yourself entertaining a sneaking admiration for his nerve. He will not let go till he pulls the whole house down with him."[5]

Wilson hoped to save the house but wasn't sure it could be done. "I am feeling the strain of things a good deal these days, with all indications pointing to a crisis in Mexico," he wrote in November 1913. "Many fateful possibilities are involved in that perplexing situation. I lie awake at night praying that the most terrible of them may be averted. No man can tell what will happen while we deal with a desperate brute like the traitor, Huerta. God save us from the worst!"[6]

To give God a hand, Wilson stepped up the pressure. He urged the governments of the other great powers to join in a campaign of ostracizing Huerta, and he provided support to Huerta's enemies. The Taft administration had imposed an embargo on arms sales to Mexican rebels; Wilson now lifted it, to the delight of the Constitutionalists. "The war will soon be over," predicted Constitutionalist general Francisco Villa, commonly called Pancho.[7]

But Villa was wrong, and Wilson was again disappointed. Huerta held on, and the fighting continued. Frustrated, Wilson nonetheless clung to the idea that Mexico might be remolded in the image of progressive America. "They say that the Mexicans are not fitted for self-government," he told a reporter, referring to faint hearts who doubted the wisdom of his insistence on Mexican democracy. "To this I reply that, when properly directed, there is no people not fitted for self-government." The idea that Mexicans could never sustain democracy was "as wickedly false as it is palpably absurd." As for the proper direction, that would come from the United States. "I hold this to be a wonderful opportunity to prove to the world that the United States of America is not only human but humane; that we are actuated by no other motives than the betterment of the conditions of our unfortunate neighbor, and by the sincere desire to advance the cause of human liberty." He confessed that his emotions were engaged. "My ideal is an orderly and righteous government in Mexico, but my passion is for the submerged eighty-five per cent of the people of that republic, who are now struggling toward liberty."[8]

Having discovered the wisdom of the Roosevelt Corollary as a theory of American hemispheric relations, Wilson now embraced the corollary as a guide to practice. In April 1914 a colonel of Huerta's forces unthinkingly arrested several American sailors who had gone ashore at Tampico. The sailors probably deserved arrest, but the colonel's superiors recognized that bigger issues were involved, and immediately released the Americans and offered an apology. Wilson refused to be satisfied. Instead he seized on the arrest as an opportunity to increase the pressure on Huerta still further. He ordered the American Atlantic fleet to converge on Tampico and the Pacific fleet to steam toward Mexico's west coast. He then went to Congress and requested authorization to "use the armed forces of the United States in such ways and to such an extent as may be necessary to obtain from General Huerta and his adherents the fullest recognition of the rights and dignity of the United States."[9]

Wilson didn't wait for Congress to say yes. His intelligence sources sent reports of the imminent arrival at Vera Cruz of a German ship carrying weapons to the Huerta government. The president thereupon ordered American troops to invade and occupy that city. The operation was successful but bloody. Nineteen Americans were killed and seventy-one wounded; the Mexican side lost more than a hundred dead and twice that many wounded.

Wilson had expected that the occupation would strengthen his own hand and weaken Huerta's, yet just the opposite occurred. Huerta's challengers had no choice but to condemn the invasion, and they did so, with evident sincerity. Nor was the condemnation confined to Mexico. In the United States, the criticism was chiefly rhetorical, but around Latin America riots broke out against American property and institutions.

Recognizing his mistake, Wilson hastily accepted an offer by Argentina, Brazil, and Chile to mediate between Washington and Mexico City. Yet this ABC solution (as American diplomats shorthanded it) was merely a tactical retreat. In a message to the three mediating governments, Wilson reiterated that the United States would accept no settlement that left Huerta anywhere near the presidential palace.

In fact, Huerta did leave office, although less as a result of the American pressure than from the growing intensity of the revolution. Caught between the Constitutionalists and the cadres of Zapata, Huerta slipped out of the country in July 1914. Shortly thereafter Carranza rode into Mexico City and proclaimed the victory of the Constitution.

After the missteps of the previous months, Wilson had reason to feel relieved. "The final working out of the situation in Mexico is still a little blind," he wrote confidentially, "but we have certainly cleared the stage and made a beginning, and with the support of thoughtful men it should be possible to hold things steady until the process is finally complete."[10]

Yet things were not so simple. Huerta's exit didn't end the revolution but rather propelled it into a new phase. The Constitutional movement fractured, with Villa taking to the mountains of the north; meanwhile the Zapatistas demanded land reform beyond anything Carranza could deliver. For his part, Carranza castigated the Americans for meddling in Mexican affairs and demanded the withdrawal of American troops.

Wilson, who thought he had done Carranza a favor by helping rid Mexico of Huerta, gnashed his teeth at the ingratitude. "I have never known of a man more impossible to deal with on human principles," he declared.[11]

Briefly Wilson flirted with Villa, which struck some of those who knew Villa as proof of Wilson's ignorance regarding Mexico; and he threatened deeper military intervention. But finally he concluded that he had no alternative to Carranza, and at the end of 1915 he accorded the Constitutionalist president grudging de facto recognition.

But even this didn't end Wilson's Mexican troubles. His embrace of Carranza prompted Villa to attack the United States in order to keep the revolutionary pot boiling. In January 1916 Villa's men captured a train traversing Sonora and killed several American miners and engineers aboard; two months later Villa's soldiers crossed into New Mexico, where they raided the town of Columbus and killed seventeen.

Wilson responded as Villa hoped, by dispatching U.S. troops into Mexico. The "Punitive Expedition," headed by General John Pershing, chased Villa hundreds of miles across northern Mexico. Carranza again had no choice but to denounce the invasion and swear to defend Mexico against American aggression. Constitutionalist troops clashed with Pershing's men.

But by this time Wilson wanted to be done with Mexico. Having discovered that revolutions don't take to dictation, even by such eloquent apostles of democracy as himself, he resisted the temptation to offer Mexico any larger instruction. Relations across the Rio Grande remained tense, and American troops remained in northern Mexico, but the threat of wider American intervention dissipated. (Even so, the lessons Wilson learned in Mexico didn't prevent him from sending troops to Haiti and the Dominican Republic, in 1915 and 1916 respectively, when trouble in those countries threatened American interests and Caribbean stability.)

Wilson's Mexican temptation would have been less resistible if not for another, far more portentous, aspect of his worldly education. During the summer of 1914, just as Carranza was coming to power in Mexico City, Wilson and America watched with horrified fascination as the powers of Europe magnified the murder of an Austrian heir into the occasion for the first continent-wide war in a century. Since the defeat of Napoleon in 1815, Europe had enjoyed a respite from general violence, becoming a model—to Americans, among others—of civilized accommodation of disputes. Not coincidentally, it was during this long period of peace that Wilson developed his enthusiasm for the British system of governance, which, especially to a southerner, had much to recommend it over an American system that had required a civil war—the most destructive conflict in the Western world during that long European peace—to settle its political disputes.

In August 1914, when the fighting in Europe began, almost no one anticipated that it would last more than several months, perhaps a year. The only real wars anyone in Europe could remember—the Franco-Prussian War of 1870–71, to cite the best example—had been sharp and short, with the statesmen firmly in control and able to halt the fighting before it got out of hand. Moreover, since then the economies of Europe had grown increasingly interdependent and the instruments of war more expensive, so that few could figure out how modern belligerents might finance a long war. With imports and exports cut off and war ministries running out of money, the armies would quickly clank to a halt.

Such thinking, combined with the traditional American aloofness from European quarrels, essentially dictated Wilson's response to the war's outbreak. In late July a reporter asked Wilson whether the United States was doing anything to slow the momentum toward war. "I can only say that the United States has never attempted to interfere in European affairs," the president responded.[12] When the fighting began, Wilson declared American neutrality.

Yet Wilson couldn't leave things at that. He felt obliged to elaborate, to explain that the neutrality he envisioned was not the narrow neutrality of international law but a higher neutrality, a neutrality of the spirit. "The people of the United States are drawn from many nations, and chiefly from the nations now at war," he told the country. "It is natural and inevitable that there should be the utmost variety of sympathy and desire among them with regard to the issues and circumstances of the conflict. Some will wish one nation, others another, to succeed in the momentous struggle. It will be easy to excite passion and difficult to allay it." This was precisely what Americans must resist, lest they be drawn inexorably into the conflict. "I venture, therefore, my fellow countrymen, to speak a solemn word of warning to you against that deepest, most subtle, most essential breach of neutrality, which may spring out of partisanship, out of passionately taking sides. The United States must be neutral in fact as well as in name during these days that are to try men's souls. We must be impartial in thought as well as in action, must put a curb upon our sentiments as well as upon every transaction that might be construed as a preference of one party to the struggle before another."[13]

As a counsel of perfection, neutrality in thought was an admirable goal; but once the fighting began in earnest, it was as difficult to maintain as Wilson warned it would be. Germany and Austria-Hungary (and, to a far lesser extent, the third of the Central Powers, Ottoman Turkey) were the warmly remembered ancestral homes of millions of Americans; but an even larger number identified by heritage with Britain and France (and, to a lesser degree, the other Allied Power, Russia). In

addition, there were those Americans whose ancestry predis-
posed them *against* one of the belligerents: Irish wishing ill to
Britain, Russian Jews rooting against the czar, Greeks hoping for
the defeat of the Turks.

Beyond the background of Americans, the behavior of the
belligerents inspired strong feelings in the United States. Apolo-
gists for Germany cited strategic reasons for the German invasion of neutral Belgium at the war's outset, but most Americans
couldn't excuse Berlin's act. And when Kaiser Wilhelm's foreign
minister dismissed the international guarantee of Belgium's neutrality—which Germany itself had signed—as a "scrap of paper,"
German arrogance became a fixture in American perceptions.
Britain's propaganda agencies amplified this perception by dis-
seminating tales of German atrocities; the spurious nature of
some of the stories eventually came out but not before they
accomplished their purpose.

Had the fighting been as brief as most analysts anticipated, all
this might have mattered no more than differing opinions on the
World Series. But the belligerents outlasted the war's first winter,
and neither side evinced any imminent need to quit. Their stay-
ing power reflected the degree to which the emotions of their
own peoples had become engaged: as the casualties mounted, the
killed and maimed became arguments not for peace but for fighting on to victory, however distant and difficult that might be.

Another reason for the war's surprising duration directly
involved the United States. The short-war scenario had been
based on the belief that when the belligerents ran out of money
they would have to put down their empty guns. In the past
this principle had generally held true. But the recent emergence
of the United States as an economic power allowed the compet-
ing war ministries to hope for American help, in the form of

American money. If dollars could be coaxed across the Atlantic, the belligerents might fight on past the time their own resources ran dry.

The French were the first to pursue this strategy. Indeed, the war wasn't a month old before Paris approached J. P. Morgan and Company about selling French bonds in the United States. The Morgan men were tickled at the prospect of the business but decided to check with the State Department to determine whether bonds for belligerents comported with the administration's definition of American national interest.

William Jennings Bryan thought not—emphatically not. Besides being a populist, and on that ground disinclined to do any favors for the Morgans of the world, the secretary of state was a pacifist. He believed that war was no inevitable aspect of international affairs but the result of specific sins on the part of powerful men. Among the sinners were those who aimed to batten on the misfortunes of war: the arms merchants and their underwriters. International law allowed trade between neutrals and belligerents but barred certain goods as contraband. Bryan now argued to Wilson that the category of contraband ought to include money. "Money," Bryan argued, "is the worst of all contrabands because it commands everything else." And leaving aside the question of morality—which was to say, complicity in the butchery—allowing the loans would endanger American neutrality. The bondholders and their agents would employ their influence to ensure the survival of their debtors. "This influence would make it all the more difficult for us to maintain neutrality," Bryan said, "as our action on various questions that would arise would affect one side or the other, and powerful financial interests would be thrown into the balance." By contrast, for the United States to deny the loans would have a decidedly pacifying effect. "We are the one great nation which is not involved, and our refusal to loan to any belligerent would naturally tend to hasten a conclusion of the war."[14]

Wilson initially let himself be persuaded by Bryan's argument and approved a ban on loans to the belligerents. But the belligerents—the French in particular—persisted. They applied for credits to be used strictly to purchase American goods. They contended that if trade with the belligerents was legal and proper, as the Wilson administration agreed it was, then credits to facilitate that trade were legal and proper, too. Moreover, as credits were a customary means of doing business, to withhold them on account of the war might actually be considered *un*neutral.

Wilson chose to accept this argument even while sticking with the larger ban on regular loans. Yet the distinction proved impossible to maintain. Dollars were dollars, whether spent on American goods or something else. In addition, an ineluctable dynamic of trade soon set in. The American economy was in recession when the war began, but the war orders from Europe quickly reeled in the slack and set American industry and agriculture humming. The credits kept the humming at an encouraging pitch—and, much as Bryan predicted, created important constituencies for whatever measures might be necessary to sustain the good times.

By the summer of 1915 it was apparent that these measures included outright loans. Britain and France were financially wracked; only a massive infusion of American money could keep them going. And their collapse, should that occur, would be America's economic disaster. "If the European countries cannot find means to pay for the excess of goods sold to them over those purchased from them, they will have to stop buying and our present export trade will shrink proportionately," wrote Robert Lansing of the State Department, who disagreed with Bryan on the loan question. "The result would be restriction of outputs, industrial depression, idle capital and idle labor, numerous failures, financial demoralization, and general unrest and suffering among the laboring classes."[15]

It was a sobering prospect, especially for a president who hoped to be reelected in little over a year. Judging that his responsibility to America included ministering to the nation's economic health, Wilson quietly withdrew his objections to belligerent loans. In the interests of continued American neutrality, he made clear that both sides might borrow money in the United States.

Both sides might, but both sides didn't, at least not anywhere near equally. From the start, American loans to the Allied Powers greatly outstripped those to the Central Powers; eventually the ratio reached ten to one. In part the difference owed to the closer ties between American banks and their British and French counterparts, as compared to German and Austrian banks; but to a much larger degree it reflected the pattern of wartime trade.

As soon as the war began, each side attempted to blockade the other. The Allies had the better luck, as a result of Britain's formidable fleet and the general difficulty of maritime access to Germany and Austria. In consequence, while American trade with Britain and France grew rapidly under the spur of the war, American trade with Germany withered.

This wasn't how things were supposed to happen, at least not from the American point of view. As a neutral, the United States should have been free to trade with both sides equally. Although traditional conceptions of contraband would have allowed the blockaders to stop shipments of guns and ammunition, other articles of trade should have passed unimpeded.

But the British, who, as inveterate blockaders, had rarely respected neutral trading rights, showed no desire to start now. They were determined to strangle Germany, and if that required violating the rights of Americans and other neutrals, they were prepared to do so. They defined contraband so broadly as to include almost anything that might support troops in the field, including food. They habitually halted American ships, boarded and searched them, and forced them into British or French ports, where their cargoes were impounded. It was all done in a very civilized manner; no one got hurt, and the owners received their ships back and were typically paid for the confiscated cargoes.

Yet the practice was insulting to American honor, and the Wilson administration protested. As one memo to London put the issue: "It is needless to point out to His Majesty's Government, usually the champion of the freedom of the seas and the rights of trade [this was a tactful fiction], that peace, not war, is the normal relation between nations, and the commerce between countries which are not belligerents should not be interfered with by those at war unless such interference is manifestly an imperative necessity to protect their national safety, and then only to the extent that it is a necessity." The note went on to describe freedom of the seas as "critical" to American merchants and shippers. "Producers and exporters, steamship and insurance companies are pressing, and not without reason, for relief from the menace to transatlantic trade which is gradually but surely destroying their business and threatening them with financial disaster." If the violations continued, they might well "arouse a feeling contrary to that which has so long existed between the American and British peoples."[16]

It was Germany's blockade of Britain and France, however, that elicited much louder protests from Washington, despite being far less effective. Britannia ruled the waves but not the waters beneath the waves, where German submarines, or U-boats, prowled. A later generation of submarines would include some of the largest, fastest, most powerful warships in the world, but Germany's pioneers were small, flimsy, and slow. They couldn't surface to give warning to potential prey lest they be raked by gunfire, rammed, or outrun. As a consequence, their only course of effective action was to torpedo enemy ships from submerged cover, typically killing some or all of the crewmen (the submarines lacked space to carry survivors, even if their commanders had wished to pick them up), not to mention destroying the ships and cargo. With reason the submarines were called "assassins of the sea."

At first the submarines targeted only warships, but as the fighting persisted and the British blockade tightened around Germany, Berlin became convinced that a submarine campaign against merchantmen was essential to Germany's survival. At the beginning of 1915 the German government declared a war zone around the British Isles, in which all Allied merchant vessels were liable to be sunk.[17] Although directed primarily at Britain and France, the German announcement gave notice to neutrals to be careful in the war zone. Neutral passengers might suffer in attacks on British or French ships, and neutral ships might find themselves accidentally targeted as a consequence of the British practice of illegally flying neutral flags.

The German announcement made the Allies' submarine problem America's problem. The mere warning raised insurance rates on American ships, keeping many vessels in port—precisely as it was intended to do. Two years earlier, Wilson wouldn't have crossed the street to protect the profits of the big companies that owned the ships and exported the goods, but as president he couldn't let the German threat pass unchallenged. He sent a note to Berlin expressing his "grave concern" at the German message, warning of the "critical situation" that would follow destruction of American vessels or loss of American life, and vowing that the United States would hold Germany to "strict accountability" for the actions of its submarine commanders.[18]

Wilson's strict-accountability policy was tested shortly. Several weeks after the German announcement, an American was killed in the sinking of the British liner *Falaba*. Three more Americans died when the American tanker *Gulflight* was hit. Even as the administration pondered its reaction to these events, a much larger provocation occurred. On May 7, 1915, a German submarine sank the British liner *Lusitania* in the Irish Sea. Nearly 1,200 persons perished, including 128 Americans. The shock of the mass killing was scarcely mitigated by reports (which turned out to be true) that the *Lusitania* was covertly carrying munitions, nor by a recently renewed warning from Germany about passenger travel in the war zone.

The *Lusitania* sinking caused a dramatic shift in American perceptions of the war. Previously, the conflict had been about other people; now it was about Americans. Before the *Lusitania* the concept of neutral rights had involved commerce and profits; now it involved American lives. As yet, very few Americans argued that their country ought to enter the war, but even fewer found entry inconceivable.

The *Lusitania* affair set off a heated debate within the Wilson administration. Edward House saw the crisis as the first in a series of provocations that wouldn't end until German power was definitively checked. "America has come to the parting of the ways," House told Wilson, "when she must determine whether she stands for civilized or uncivilized warfare. . . . We can no longer remain neutral spectators."[19]

William Jennings Bryan interpreted things differently. Convinced that a sharp American reaction would lead to war, which would simply compound the insanity that had seized the world, the secretary of state recommended that passengers be barred from ships carrying munitions. Bryan reminded Wilson that the British violated American rights more consistently, if less egregiously, than the Germans. If the administration insisted on American neutral rights vis-à-vis Germany, it must do the same regarding Britain.

Wilson was torn. The thought of war appalled him, especially if it came over such a minor point as the right of Americans to travel on belligerent ships. At the same time, he knew he had to draw the line somewhere against foreign aggression. Perhaps this was the place.

While he was formulating his official reaction, he traveled to Philadelphia to address a group of newly naturalized citizens. There he tested an idea he evidently had been pondering for some time. "Americans must have a consciousness different from the consciousness of every other nation in the world," he said. "The example of America must be a special example. The example of America must be the example, not merely of peace because it will not fight, but of peace because peace is the healing and elevating influence of the world, and strife is not. There is such a thing as a man being too proud to fight. There is such a thing as a nation being so right that it does not need to convince others by force that it is right."[20]

For once Wilson's words betrayed him. What did it mean for a nation to be "too proud to fight" when 128 of its people lay dead on the ocean floor? Even the many Americans who still hoped to keep their country clear of the war wondered whether this president was up to the job.

Wilson himself realized he had misspoken. "I have a bad habit of thinking out loud," he confessed to a friend the day after his too-proud-to-fight speech. "That thought occurred to me while I was speaking, and I let it out. I should have kept it in, or developed it further, of course."[21] To reporters he offered a disclaimer: "I was expressing a personal attitude, that was all. I did not really have in mind any specific thing."[22]

Second thought produced the administration's official response. Dismissing the idea that the *Lusitania*'s cargo in any way mitigated the crime of its sinking, Wilson dispatched a note to Berlin declaring, "The principal fact is that a great steamer, primarily and chiefly a conveyance for passengers, and carrying more than a thousand souls who had no part or lot in the conduct of the war, was torpedoed and sunk without so much as a challenge or a warning, and that men, women, and children were sent to their death in circumstances unparalleled in modern warfare." The tragic circumstance that more than one hundred of those killed were Americans made it the particular concern of the United States. But the principle had broader applicability and far transcended the issues that till now had vexed U.S.-German relations. "The Government of the United States is contending for something much greater than mere rights of property or privileges of commerce. It is contending for nothing less high and sacred than the rights of humanity."[23] Accordingly, Wilson insisted that Germany change its submarine policy and give assurances that such attacks would not recur.

Berlin mumbled in reply, citing the complexities of submarine warfare and the extenuating circumstances of British malfeasance. Wilson rejected the response as "very unsatisfactory" and sharpened the American position. "Illegal and inhuman acts, however justifiable they may be thought to be against an enemy who is believed to have acted in contravention of law and humanity, are manifestly indefensible when they deprive neutrals of their acknowledged rights, particularly when they violate the right to life itself." For Germany to persist in the policies that led to the *Lusitania* sinking would constitute an "unpardonable offense" against American sovereignty; another such action would be construed as "deliberately unfriendly" to the United States.[24]

This strong wording came at a price to Wilson: the loss of Bryan, who opposed the stern policy to the end. Wilson tried to mollify him. "I hope that you will realize how hard it goes with me to differ with you in judgment about such grave matters as we are now handling," he told Bryan. "You always have such weight of reason, as well as such high motives, behind what you urge that it is with deep misgiving that I turn from what you press upon me."[25]

But Bryan wouldn't be mollified. He reiterated that the president's message cast American neutrality into serious doubt; he also complained that Wilson paid less heed to him, the secretary of state, than to House, a private citizen. "Colonel House," Bryan told Wilson in what amounted to his exit interview, "has been secretary of state, not I, and I have never had your full confidence."[26]

This was true enough, but it wouldn't help Wilson for it to become public knowledge at this delicate moment. When Bryan formally submitted his letter of resignation, Wilson replied in rather ungracious language. "My feeling about your retirement from the Secretaryship of State goes so much deeper than regret," he wrote. "I sincerely deplore it."[27] And well he might have, for even as he moved closer to war with Germany, Bryan's defection gave the antiwar elements in the country a tested champion.

The break with Bryan may have been inevitable, but it could have been handled better. That it wasn't was due partly to Wilson's peculiar aloofness: his inability or unwillingness to make the personal connections that come naturally to more gregarious types and smooth the path of born politicians. The breakup with Bryan was due also to the disordered state of Wilson's mind—and heart—at this particular moment.

Wilson had married in 1885. His wife was the former Ellen Axson, the daughter of a Presbyterian minister of Rome, Georgia, where Wilson had relatives. For the twenty-nine years after their wedding, Woodrow and Ellen Wilson's marriage proceeded fruitfully—they had three children, all daughters—but unremarkably. He confided his hopes and dreams to Ellen, and loved her dearly, although at one point during the late Princeton period he had an extramarital affair of sorts with a woman named Mary Peck, whom he encountered at Bermuda while on vacation. Precisely what passed between Wilson and Mary Peck is impossible to say, but an embarrassed Wilson later referred to it as "the contemptible error and madness of a few months."[28] If Ellen suspected anything, she didn't let on. She supported his turn from academics to politics, and she was pleased to become First Lady in 1913. But during the initial year of his presidency she developed kidney disease, which was complicated by a bad fall. She declined rapidly during the summer of 1914 and died on August 6.

The loss of Ellen devastated her husband. Associates who knew Wilson chiefly as the self-contained intellectual were amazed at the emotion that now burst forth. "Oh, my God! What am I to do?" Wilson moaned.[29] He sobbed inconsolably at the funeral. Afterward the family physician, Cary Grayson, found him in the White House, sitting alone, tears streaming down his face. "A sadder picture, no one could imagine," Grayson recorded. "A great man with his heart torn out."[30]

In losing Ellen, Wilson lost his closest confidante, the one person in all the world to whom he really unburdened himself. He and House were close politically, and at times their relationship approached genuine friendship. But both men recognized that, in the end, theirs was a friendship of convenience, and this recognition always colored their dealings.

Yet despite his difficulty in making friends—or perhaps because of it—Wilson craved the support emotional intimacy entails. Wilson was a man who came to conclusions not by reason but by intuition; he simply *knew* certain things were true. Needless to say, his intuition was no help to critics whose sensibilities were differently tuned. And the more critics he encountered, the more he needed the support of those who didn't question his conclusions. House was shrewd enough to keep his doubts to himself, but Ellen positively believed that her husband could do no wrong. Her death, which came just as Europe went to war and Wilson entered the most trying portion of his presidency, left him with no one who offered the unquestioning loyalty and support that gave him the courage to carry on.

At times he didn't want to carry on. House dined with Wilson one evening and described the engagement in his diary: "His face became grey and he looked positively sick. I was unable to lift him out of this depression before bedtime. He said he was broken in spirit by Mrs. Wilson's death, and was not fit to be President because he did not think straight any longer, and had no heart in the things he was doing."[31] A week later Wilson visited New York and insisted on taking a nighttime walk through the darkened streets. House tagged along, worried about the president's well-being. "When we reached home, he began to tell me how lonely and sad his life was since Mrs. Wilson's death, and he could not help wishing when we were out tonight that someone would kill him. He has told me this before. His eyes were moist when he spoke of not wanting to live longer, and of not being fit to do the work he had in hand."[32]

Wilson remained depressed for months, through the end of 1914 and into the following year. His work would distract him for a time, but then he would slip back into his despair. What finally snapped him out of it was not any insight into the meaning of life and death but a pretty face and an attractive figure. One afternoon in February 1915, as he and Dr. Grayson were riding down Connecticut Avenue, Grayson waved at a woman on the sidewalk. "Who is that beautiful lady?" the president inquired.[33]

She was Edith Bolling Galt, an acquaintance of Grayson's and the widow of a man whose family owned Washington's poshest jewelry store. In the seven years since his death, she had acquired control of the business, which provided her a comfortably independent living and entrée to the most exclusive salons of the capital city. She lived in a house near Dupont Circle, from which she ventured forth by foot and automobile. Driving her own car, she prided herself on being the first Washington woman to indulge such daring.

Out of no disrespect for the memory of Ellen—only six months dead—but rather out of concern for the president's emotional health, Grayson arranged an introduction. Wilson found Edith enchanting. A Virginian like himself, she listened avidly while he read poetry to her, discussed affairs of state, and made the small talk that marks the smitten. In April she sat in the presidential box while Wilson threw out the pitch that opened the Washington Senators' home season.

Wilson had been distracted by Ellen's death, but the entry of Edith into his life sent him into a tizzy. He saw her whenever he could, and wrote her when he couldn't—often two or three times a day. Not even the most pressing public business kept him from his reveries about Edith; if anything, it was the other way around. After his faux pas in the *Lusitania* crisis, when he talked of being too proud to fight, he explained to Edith that it was the result of a meeting they'd had the day before. "I do not know just what I said at Philadelphia (as I rode along the street in the dusk I found myself a little confused as to whether I was in Philadelphia or New York!) because my heart was in such a whirl from that wonderful interview of yesterday and the poignant appeal and sweetness of the little note you left with me."[34] As Bryan was preparing to leave the cabinet, Wilson seemed at least as worried about the arrival of a houseguest at Edith's, whose presence would inhibit the intimacy of their moments together. And during the days when he was drafting and dispatching his *Lusitania* ultimatum to Germany, he put far more of himself into his letters to Edith.

I simply *must* write to you every minute I am free to. It is just as instinctive with me, and just as necessary to me, as

if you were here in the house and I were free for a little
while to go and hold you in my arms and pour out to you
everything that was in my mind or heart. . . . What
thoughts of you fill and gladden my heart, my Sweetheart!
How deep I have drunk of the sweet fountains of love that
are in you—and how pure and wholesome and refreshing
they are, how full of life and every sweet perfection! . . .
Ah, how I need you! How empty the hours are without
you! I can make shift while the working hours last; but
when they are over, when there is time and opportunity
for a touch of *home*—when bed-time comes and you are
not here to crown the day with sweet sympathy and ten-
derness and comprehension of my need, how I get by these
crises I do not know—how often, how long I shall be able
to get by them I dare not try to think or reckon![35]

Edith was flattered by the attention—and by the access to the
inner workings of power. She was fascinated by what Wilson
told her of his political and diplomatic affairs, and her fascination caused him to tell her more. He sent copies of government
correspondence to her house, for her examination. After some
initial diffidence, she began offering advice. She didn't like
Bryan, and when he left the administration she was positively
gleeful. "Hurrah! old Bryan is out!" she wrote Wilson. "I could
shout and sing that at last the world will *know* just what he is."[36]
Not surprisingly, the unexpected emergence of this newcomer at Wilson's side occasioned concern among the president's associates, every one of whom faced demotion by at least
a notch. But after seeing Wilson sunk in despair for months,
even House, whose position was the most threatened, was

pleased that Edith had restored the president's taste for life and work. When Wilson mentioned marriage, some of his advisers sought to postpone it till after the 1916 election, lest voters take amiss the rush to remarriage. But once Edith consented, Wilson wouldn't hear of delay. In October 1915 the White House announced the engagement; in December the small wedding was held at Edith's home. The departing couple drove a confusing route through Washington to elude reporters, then honeymooned at Hot Springs, Virginia.

The public, apparently more tolerant of a man in love than Wilson's handlers had feared, didn't conspicuously disapprove. This was convenient, as the end of the honeymoon marked the beginning of Wilson's campaign for a second term. In the depths of his mourning for Ellen, he had considered stepping down after a single term, but with new love came new hope and rekindled ambition. Indeed, so interested was Edith in presidential affairs that he would have felt he was letting her down had he not run. And he was still sufficiently infatuated that he would have done nearly anything not to let her down.

Although domestic issues—especially those addressed by the New Freedom—demanded voters' attention in the 1916 campaign, from the outset it was apparent that the European war, and America's relation to it, would have much to do with whether Wilson won reelection. And despite the genuine outrage that had followed the *Lusitania* sinking, it was obvious that the American people wanted to stay clear of the war. So did Wilson, even as some of his advisers, particularly House and the new secretary of state, Robert Lansing, were growing convinced that the United States would have to join the fighting. Wilson hoped that a combination of firmness and restraint could persuade the

Germans—and, less crucially, the British—to respect American rights without the need for American belligerence.

He had reason for his hope. Amid the *Lusitania* crisis, the German admiralty issued secret orders to its submarine commanders not to target passenger ships. One commander violated orders, either inadvertently or otherwise, and attacked the British passenger vessel *Arabic.* Two Americans died in the attack. The anger in America convinced the German ambassador, Johann Bernstorff, that a rupture was imminent; to forestall a break, Bernstorff revealed the new policy. His action earned him a rebuke from Berlin but served to defuse the anger, and the so-called *Arabic* pledge—that German submarines would not attack passenger ships without warning and provision for the safety of civilians—gave Wilson breathing space.

But that space was subject to the vicissitudes of war, which included many foggy days in the waters around Britain. Submarine commanders couldn't always distinguish passenger ships from cargo ships, especially when the British and French took pains to blur the difference. In March 1916 the French-flagged ferry *Sussex* was torpedoed in the English Channel. It didn't sink, but the explosion caused scores of casualties, including four Americans wounded. The German government initially denied responsibility, saying the ship had struck a mine, of which the British had sown thousands in nearby waters.

To those disposed to think the worst of Germany, the *Sussex* attack seemed patent evidence of Berlin's duplicity. House and Lansing urged Wilson to respond in the strongest terms, arguing that anything less would give the impression of fatal weakness in Washington. "I do not see how we can avoid taking some decisive step," Lansing told Wilson. "We can no longer temporize in the matter of submarine warfare when Americans are being killed, wounded, or endangered by the illegal and inhuman conduct of the Germans."[37]

But Wilson had reasons for temporizing. From the standpoint of diplomacy, he had yet to be convinced that war was either inevitable or necessary; from the standpoint of politics, he had no desire to campaign on a war platform until voters were thoroughly ready for war. It was chiefly politics that caused him to answer the *Sussex* sinking in another speech to a joint session of Congress. Recapitulating the course of German policy during the last year, the president asserted, "Tragedy has followed tragedy on the seas in such fashion, with such attendant circumstances, as to make it grossly evident that warfare of such a sort, if warfare it be, cannot be carried on without the most palpable violation of the dictates alike of right and of humanity." The government of the United States had been patient. "It has been willing to wait until the significance of the facts became absolutely unmistakable and susceptible of but one interpretation." Pausing for emphasis, he went on, "That point has now unhappily been reached." Germany had shown that it could not wage submarine warfare except by means "incompatible with the principles of humanity, the long established and incontrovertible rights of neutrals, and the sacred immunities of noncombatants." This being so, the United States was forced to deliver an ultimatum: "Unless the Imperial German Government should now immediately declare and effect an abandonment of its present methods of warfare against passenger and freight-carrying vessels, this Government can have no choice but to sever diplomatic relations."[38]

Under the circumstances, few could doubt that a severing of relations would lead to war. Germany, at any rate, so interpreted Wilson's warning and backed off. In May 1916 Berlin promised not to attack unresisting merchant vessels without providing for the safety of passengers and crew.[39] At the same time, however, it suggested that unless the United States reciprocated by forcing Britain to ease its blockade, the attacks might resume.

Lansing feared a trick. "The more I study the reply the less I like it," he told Wilson. "It has all the elements of the 'gold brick' swindle with a decidedly insolent tone."[40] But the president was in no mood for war over the niceties of language—because he knew the American people weren't. Seizing on the German promise, while ignoring the conditions, he presented the *Sussex* pledge as a triumph for American—which was to say Wilsonian—diplomacy.

In doing so he borrowed trouble, but he guessed that repayment wouldn't be required till after the election. His campaign theme was "He kept us out of war," and it sufficed to keep Wilson in the White House. Yet the race was excruciatingly close. The Republicans nominated Charles Evans Hughes, formerly governor of New York and recently Supreme Court justice. Hughes benefited from the healing of his party's 1912 rift; even Theodore Roosevelt endorsed him. Wilson, however, had the advantages of incumbency and of a friendly Congress. The latter had been busy delivering legislation progressives had sought for some time: banning most child labor, mandating an eight-hour day for railroad workers, establishing an inheritance tax. And, as always, Wilson had the advantage of his way with words. After one rally, an impressed but not entirely approving *New York Times* was inspired to remark, "The President has been renowned for the intellectual quality of his speeches. Yesterday he took his place beside the other great leaders of his party who have won fame for their ability to play on the emotion of their hearers."[41]

Even so, on election night Wilson's eloquence appeared to have fallen short. He went to bed behind in the balloting and woke up to read papers proclaiming Hughes the next president. But late returns from the West eroded Hughes's lead, and in the following days Wilson nosed in front. He finally won by a margin of 23 electoral votes and not quite 700,000 popular votes.

3

---

# More Precious than Peace

Like most presidents, Wilson hoped reelection would free him from some of the constraints of politics, as he would no longer have to court voters for the next election. To be sure, the hex on third terms wasn't what it had been before Theodore Roosevelt broke the informal ban on trying for more than eight years, but Roosevelt's experience hardly augured well for imitators. Even so, upon his second inauguration, Wilson—and the American people—had every reason to believe that history, rather than the voters, would now be his judge.

Yet if the political shackles fell away, diplomacy gripped him tighter than ever. By his reaction to the *Sussex* sinking, he had handed to Germany effective control over America's fate. If Berlin resumed the submarine campaign, Wilson would have to sever relations and almost certainly ask Congress for war. To do less would require him to go back on his word—a word he had insisted on giving in the most public forum he could command—and would give the lie to all the noble principles he had expounded.

Wilson appreciated the delicacy of his situation, and it prompted him to try to end the war before Germany felt compelled to take the step that would force his hand. Even before the *Sussex* incident he had tried to coax the belligerents to the peace table. He sent House to England, where the Texan conferred with British foreign secretary Edward Grey. House remained disposed toward American belligerence; Grey preferred not belligerence per se—which would have required Britain to accommodate American interests—but rather the threat of belligerence. The two concocted a scheme that was both devious and ineffectual, yet nonetheless revealed the direction in which affairs were inexorably trending. House and Grey drafted a memorandum of understanding, dated February 22, 1916, to the effect that on the advice of Britain and France, the United States would call for a peace conference among all the belligerents. If Germany refused, "the United States would probably enter the war against Germany." If the conference met and failed to reach a settlement, "the United States would leave the conference as a belligerent on the side of the Allies, if Germany was unreasonable."[1]

The House-Grey memorandum was fraught with difficulties. It ignored the fact that the American president couldn't declare war by himself; Congress had to approve a presidential request for war, and Congress wasn't about to approve any such thing in advance. It also gave entirely too much influence to the Allies. Britain and France would control the timing of an American call for a peace conference; they certainly wouldn't do so until the moment they judged conditions on the battlefield most propitious for a conference that favored them—at which moment Germany would be least likely to agree to a brokered peace. And what did "unreasonable" mean in the context of a failed conference?

Despite the problems, Wilson accepted the House-Grey memorandum, adding only another "probably" in the clause about the United States leaving a failed conference on the side of the Allies.[2] He appreciated the deficiencies of the document, but at a time when he lacked other leverage with either the Allies or Germany, even this little was worth something. If nothing else, it put the Allies on record as contemplating a peace short of German surrender, a peace without victory.

It was this last consideration that prompted Wilson to try again, after nothing came of the House-Grey plan. In December 1916 he requested that the opposing sides state the conditions on which they would be willing to make peace. When the antagonists, not surprisingly, refused to tip their hands, Wilson proceeded to tell them what those conditions ought to be. "First of all . . . ," he said, "it must be a peace without victory." Wilson conceded that this would go down hard with peoples who had sacrificed so much. But any other sort of peace would never last. "Victory would mean peace forced upon the loser, a victor's terms imposed upon the vanquished. It would be accepted in humiliation, under duress, at an intolerable sacrifice, and would leave a sting, a resentment, a bitter memory upon which terms of peace would rest, not permanently, but only as upon quicksand." Second, any permanent peace required the enlargement of the area of self-government. "No peace can last, or ought to last, which does not recognize and accept the principle that governments derive all their just powers from the consent of the governed." Third, freedom of the seas must be guaranteed; it was "the *sine qua non* of peace." Fourth, arms must be controlled and limited. "The question of armaments, whether on land or sea, is the most immediately and intensely practical question connected with the future fortunes of nations and mankind." Finally, any durable settlement must include provisions for a "League of Peace," an international body with the power to enforce good behavior among nations. Peace in the past had been based on a balance of power among potential antagonists—and had been found wanting, as the present war revealed. Future peace must be based on something broader. "There must be, not a balance of power, but a community of power; not organized rivalries, but an organized common peace."[3]

Wilson conceded that he was demanding a lot. But he believed he was in a unique position to do so. "Perhaps I am the only person in high authority amongst all the peoples of the world who is at liberty to speak and hold nothing back. I am speaking as an individual, and yet I am speaking also, of course, as the responsible head of a great government, and I feel confident that I have said what the people of the United States would wish me to say." Nor the people of the United States alone. "May I not add that I hope and believe that I am in effect speaking for liberals and friends of humanity in every nation and of every program of liberty? I would fain believe that I am speaking for the silent mass of mankind everywhere who have as yet had no place or opportunity to speak their real hearts out concerning the death and ruin they see to have come already upon the persons and the homes they hold most dear." The principles he espoused would serve both America and humanity at large. "These are American principles, American policies. We could stand for no others. And they are also the principles and policies of forward-looking men and women everywhere, of every modern nation, of every enlightened community. They are the principles of mankind and must prevail."[4]

Wilson's words elicited broad and often enthusiastic approval in the United States. "We have just passed through a very important hour in the life of the world," said Senator Robert La Follette of Wisconsin. Senator John Shafroth of Colorado declared,

"It was the greatest message of a century." The *New York Times* proclaimed, "This is not merely a guarantee of peace, it is a moral transformation." The *New Republic* chimed, "It will be something to boast of that we have lived in a time when the world called us into partnership, and we went gladly, went remembering what we had always professed, and pledged ourselves to it in a larger theatre. At least it shall not be said that we were too selfish and too timid to attempt it, or that the sources of American idealism have run dry."[5]

The applause was premature. On January 31, 1917, Berlin announced that it was launching an unrestricted submarine offensive. In the waters around the British Isles, all vessels—belligerent and neutral, naval and civilian—would be subject to attack. For many months the German government had been split between those generals and admirals who wanted to tighten the noose around England, even at the risk of American belligerence, and those diplomats who believed American entry would doom German hopes of victory. By the beginning of 1917 the latter group, under the pressure of Britain's blockade and the attrition of the trench fighting, could no longer fend off the former. The German announcement represented a grand gamble: that German troops could defeat the British and French before the Americans arrived in large enough numbers to determine the outcome.

The German announcement hit Wilson hard. "The President was sad and depressed, and I did not succeed at any time during the day in lifting him into a better frame of mind," House recorded in his diary for February 1. "He was deeply disappointed at the sudden and unwarranted action of the German Government." Wilson had thought his peace proposals were having a positive effect, but this latest news proved him wrong. "The President said he felt as if the world had suddenly reversed itself; that after going from east to west, it had begun to go from west to east and that he could not get his balance."[6]

The German action left Wilson no choice but to break relations. As he explained to Congress in announcing the break, "This Government has no alternative consistent with the dignity and honor of the United States." Yet he refused to concede that war was inevitable. "We do not desire any hostile conflict with the Imperial German Government. We are the sincere friends of the German people and earnestly desire to remain at peace with the Government which speaks for them. We shall not believe that they are hostile to us unless and until we are obliged to believe it."[7]

Wilson was obliged to believe it soon enough—but not before two unforeseen events made hostilities more palatable than they had been. In late February, the British government handed the State Department a telegram it had intercepted, from the German foreign minister Arthur Zimmermann to the German embassy in Mexico, proposing an alliance between Germany and Mexico (and Japan, currently an ally of Britain and France) against the United States. The troubles between the United States and Mexico hadn't quite ended; beyond weighing in against Wilson on these current events, Berlin offered to help Mexico regain the territory it lost in the war of 1846–48. The Mexicans weren't seriously tempted by such a ludicrous scheme (neither, for different reasons, did the Japanese think much of the German plan), and the chief result of the Zimmermann telegram, after Wilson made it public, was to increase American anger at Germany.

The second event was more distant but far more portentous. In March 1917 (February by the local, Orthodox calendar), Russia erupted in revolution. The czar was overthrown and a provisional representative government established. None could know at this point that the provisional government was simply a way station en route to a regime more despotic than the old, but most in the West greeted it hopefully. For Wilson, the replacement of the czar eliminated one of the arguments against American belligerence. So long as the Allies included the regime of the Russian czar, Wilson couldn't contend that a blow for the Allies was automatically a blow for democracy. If anything, the czar's government was more reactionary than that of Germany. But with the fall of the czar and the birth of Russian republicanism, the moral case for intervention on the side of the Allies became much clearer.

The Germans all but clinched the argument by torpedoing American ships. During the week after the news from Russia, German U-boats sank three American vessels, killing fifteen. Wilson still struggled to find an alternative to war but discovered nothing. "I felt that he was resisting the irresistible logic of events," Robert Lansing wrote, after meeting with the president, "and that he resented being compelled to abandon the neutral position which had been preserved with so much difficulty."[8] Wilson summoned the cabinet and polled the members for their advice. All agreed that war was necessary, having in fact been started by the Germans. Some suggested that the American public would compel the administration to go to war, even against the president's wishes. "I do not care for popular demand," Wilson replied. "I want to do right, whether popular or not."[9] Wilson withheld his decision at this meeting, but his mood was plain. "President was solemn, very sad!!" noted Navy Secretary Daniels in his diary that night.[10]

Wilson revealed his decision soon enough. Once more summoning Congress to a joint session, he addressed the two houses on April 2. He retraced the efforts of his administration to preserve the peace while defending neutral rights against German violations; these efforts, finally and tragically, had failed. As president of the United States, he had no alternative to requesting a declaration of war.

Yet even while asking for war, Wilson sought to enhance the prospects of a future peace. The German government had revealed its utter disregard for the most basic aspiration of humanity, the desire for liberty and self-government, leaving America to rise forthrightly to humanity's defense. "We are now about to accept the gage of battle with this natural foe to liberty and shall, if necessary, spend the whole force of the nation to check and nullify its pretensions and its power. We are glad, now that we see the facts with no veil of false pretense about them, to fight thus for the ultimate peace of the world and for the liberation of its peoples." No war aims were ever more just, no conflict more righteous.

The world must be made safe for democracy. Its peace must be planted upon the tested foundations of political liberty. We have no selfish ends to serve. We desire no conquest, no dominion. We seek no indemnities for ourselves, no material compensation for the sacrifices we shall freely make. We are but one of the champions of mankind. We shall be satisfied when those rights have been made as secure as the faith and the freedom of nations can make them.

Americans faced many months of trial and sacrifice. It was a fearful thing to lead a great people into war, the most terrible war in history.

But the right is more precious than peace, and we shall fight for the things which we have always carried nearest our hearts—for our democracy, for the right of those who submit to authority to have a voice in their own governments, for the rights and liberties of small nations, for a universal dominion of right by such a concert of free peoples as shall bring peace and safety to all nations and make the world itself free at last. . . . America is privileged to spend her blood and her might for the principles that gave her birth and happiness and the peace which she has treasured. God helping her, she can do no other.[11]

Congress overwhelmingly approved Wilson's request for a war declaration, although some senators and representatives questioned the sweep of his idealism. And even among those who voted in favor, there were questions whether Wilson had the stuff to lead the nation into battle. Almost nothing in his background had prepared him to be commander in chief. He had never served in the military, opting out of the one war of his adulthood, the Spanish-American War (which had made Theodore Roosevelt famous). His study of politics had largely excluded war. His sensibilities were closer to pacifism than belligerence; odes to peace flowed naturally from his tongue and pen, while the praise of war would always be a struggle.

Wilson's politics, too, were antithetical to war, or at least he thought so before April 1917. The liberal spirit of progressivism seemed diametrically opposed to the stern mind-set required of a nation at war. Belligerence, he believed, would put everything he stood for at risk. "Every reform we have won will be lost if we go into this war," he told Josephus Daniels in 1914.[12]

Had the nation gone to war in 1914, Wilson might have been right. But by 1917 the reforms of his first administration had fairly well taken hold and weren't to be easily undone. And indeed, to an extent Wilson couldn't have anticipated, the war actually furthered the progressive program—parts of it, at any rate.

The chief difference, originally, between Wilson's New Freedom and Roosevelt's New Nationalism had been the uneasiness of Wilson and his followers with big government, as compared to the Roosevelt crowd. With Wilson's acceptance of the principle behind the Federal Trade Commission, that difference diminished. Wilson discovered—in the way presidents typically do—that power isn't nearly as threatening when wielded by oneself as when one's opponents hold it. The onset of the war continued the accretion of power under the Democratic administration and effectively completed Wilson's conversion to the New Nationalism.

To facilitate the war effort, new federal agencies and offices were established. Under a progressive administration, many of these agencies were naturally headed by progressives, who turned their progressive techniques to the prosecution of the war. The Committee on Public Information, for example, which was given responsibility for drumming up enthusiasm for the war, was directed by George Creel, a well-known muckraker, who hired such kindred pens as Ida Tarbell and Ray Stannard Baker. Relying on the progressive principle of motivation through public education, the CPI set about educating the public to the necessity of supporting the war. It unleashed a small army of "four-minute men" to speak wherever people gathered, to explain the aims of the war and the need for the American people to lend their unstinting support.

Another new agency, the War Industries Board, took charge of the logistics of war production. In certain respects, the WIB was the Federal Trade Commission in mufti. The board brought together the chieftains of America's leading industries and trade unions to hammer out agreements meant to maximize industrial production destined for the front. In deference to lingering New Freedom fears of omnivorous government, the powers of the WIB were mostly hortatory, but these proved sufficient to snap American industry into marching step, especially since they were combined with the promise of suspension of antitrust prosecution. Wilson's thinking on this latter point was plain. "He remarked that if we attempted at that moment to vindicate the law, we would disorganize industry," Attorney General Thomas Gregory recorded. "We both agreed that we should let up on these people so that they would have no excuse for not contributing to their full capacities in the prosecution of the war." Writing some years later, Gregory summarized, "We let the cases go to sleep until the war was over."[13]

The spur of the war meanwhile hastened the transition of the federal tax regime from the tariff to the income tax. Hoping to pay for as much of the war as possible out of current revenues (rather than borrowing against future revenues), Wilson persuaded Congress to raise income-tax rates and to supplement income taxes with an excess-profits tax and other levies on the wealthy. The result was remarkable: before the war, three-quarters of federal revenues derived from the tariff and excise taxes; after the war, three-quarters came from income and estate taxes.[14] Whatever else they thought of the war, the progressives had to concede that the conflict was a powerful engine of reform on taxes, putting into practice the progressive idea that those most able to pay should in fact pay the most.

The growth in federal power, however, had a darker side—the side Wilson had feared before taking office. Even as the CPI rallied Americans behind the war effort, the Justice Department hounded those who wouldn't come along. The Sedition Act of 1918 prohibited "disloyal, profane, scurrilous, or abusive language about the form of government of the United States, or the uniform of the Army or Navy," as well as any language that tended to bring the government or the military "into contempt, scorn, contumely, or disrepute."[15] As the sedition law and its companion, the 1917 Espionage Act, were eagerly enforced by Attorney General Gregory and his successor, A. Mitchell Palmer, the measures effectively stifled questioning of the wisdom of the war or the high-mindedness of American leaders. The socialist and labor leader Eugene Debs, for one, was arrested for opposing the draft and spent the duration of the war (and more) in federal prison. Radical unionists of the Industrial Workers of the World were jailed, and many of them were deported. To assist in the regimentation, the Justice Department enlisted the quasi-official American Protective League, whose 250,000 members spied on their neighbors and reported activity deemed insufficiently enthusiastic regarding the war.

In certain respects, the most coercive aspect of the wartime growth of federal power was the military draft. Champ Clark spoke for his own state and many people elsewhere when he said, "In the estimation of Missourians, there is precious little difference between a conscript and a convict."[16] Before the war, Wilson was inclined to agree with Clark, but he soon changed his mind. Officials of the War Department convinced him that reliance on volunteers would never yield the kind of coordinated mobilization the country required. Volunteers had sufficed in the Spanish-American War, although even in that minor conflict the losses due to poor planning and inadequate logistics were appalling. But Germany wasn't Spain, and the current war demanded coordination only conscription could deliver.

There was another reason for Wilson's rethinking of the draft. For months before America entered the war, Theodore Roosevelt had been planning to reprise his heroic role from the Spanish-American War, but on a grander scale. He would raise a division (rather than a regiment) of volunteers, modeled on the Rough Riders and composed of the finest specimens of American manhood. Only days after the American declaration, he came calling at the White House to ask Wilson's permission to lead the troops to France and into battle.

The meeting began awkwardly. For many months Roosevelt, who was even more anti-German than Lansing and House, had been publicly criticizing Wilson for slowness to respond to German provocation; in private—although his words doubtless found their way to Wilson—he had condemned the president as a coward and a hypocrite. But now he came, hat in hand, to request the permission only Wilson could give.

"Mr. President," he declared, "what I have said and thought, and what others have said and thought, is all dust in a windy street, if we can now make your message"—Wilson's war message—"good. Of course, it amounts to nothing if we cannot make it good. But if we can translate it into fact, then it will rank as a great state paper, with the great state papers of Washington and Lincoln."[17]

Wilson eyed Roosevelt warily. "The President doesn't like Theodore Roosevelt and he was not one bit effusive in his greeting," recorded presidential assistant Thomas Brahany. Yet Roosevelt's flattery and natural ebullience gradually eroded Wilson's reserve. "The interview lasted twenty-five minutes," Brahany continued, "and before it closed the President had thawed out and was laughing and 'talking back.' They had a real good visit." Wilson thought so, too. "I was, as formerly, charmed by his personality," Wilson told Joseph Tumulty. "There is a sweetness about him that is very compelling. You can't resist the man. I can easily understand why his followers are so fond of him." (Tumulty was quite taken by Roosevelt as well. Passing through the secretary's office, Roosevelt clapped him on the back and said, "By Jove, Tumulty, you are a man after my own heart! Six children, eh?"—Roosevelt also had six—"Well, now, you get me across and I will put you on my staff, and you may tell Mrs. Tumulty that I will not allow them to place you at any point of danger." Tumulty volunteered his opinion of Roosevelt to Wilson: "I told the President of the very favorable impression the Colonel had made upon me by his buoyancy, charm of manner, and his great good nature.")[18]

Yet for all his charm, Roosevelt failed to win Wilson's approval for his volunteer force. Although Charles Evans Hughes had been the Republican nominee in 1916, Roosevelt, now returned to the Republican fold, was once again the lion of the GOP. To let him command a division in France risked handing him the presidency in 1920. Wilson had no desire to do any such thing. And the easiest way to prevent it was to prohibit the raising of volunteer divisions. "It would be very agreeable to me to pay Mr. Roosevelt this compliment and the Allies the compliment of sending to their aid one of our most distinguished public men, an ex-President who has rendered many conspicuous public services and proved his gallantry in many striking ways," Wilson announced, the butter barely warming in his mouth. "But this is not the time or the occasion for compliment or for any action not calculated to contribute to the immediate success of the war. The business now in hand is undramatic, practical, and of scientific definiteness and precision."[19] Volunteer divisions might be colorful and glorious, but they would steal officers and men required by the regular army. There would be no Rough Riders in the war against Germany. The country would rely on conscription—although Wilson declined to label it as such. "It is in no sense a conscription of the unwilling," he declared. "It is, rather, selection from a nation which has volunteered in mass."[20]

As important as the matter of how to raise the soldiers was what to do with them once raised. In his war message of April 2, Wilson had promised "the utmost practicable cooperation" with Britain and France, but what this meant remained to be determined.[21]

The British and French thought they knew: they wanted American troops sent over at once and thrown into the holes in the British and French lines created by German artillery, mines, machine guns, and gas. This course promised the most rapid reinforcement of the anti-German front, as the Americans wouldn't have to train entire divisions but only individual soldiers, who would serve under British and French officers. Amalgamation of the Americans into the existing Allied armies would also obviate the duplication and competition that would be bound to arise if the Americans came in as a distinct and self-sufficient army.

Predictably, American military officers rebelled at the suggestion of handing their troops over to the same British and French commanders who had squandered their own soldiers by the hundreds of thousands. General Pershing, recalled from Mexico to head the preparations for the fighting in Europe, refused even to consider the Allied requests, and did his best to prevent Wilson's considering them. Pershing cited the proven ineptitude of the Allied commanders, the likely unwillingness of American soldiers to fight under foreign officers, and the language problems with the French. Looking toward the war's end, he added, "Our position will be stronger if our army, acting as such, shall have played a distinct and definite part."[22]

This last argument was decisive for Wilson. Not unusually for one who knew so little of war, the president was more interested in the shape of the peace than in the conduct of the war. He was happy to defer to Pershing—and to War Secretary Newton Baker, who took the same line regarding the Allies as Pershing—on the issue of amalgamation; such a course would free his hand for the peace conference that would follow the war.

The wisdom of this approach became especially apparent in the autumn of 1917. The Russian Revolution had moved into its second stage, in which the Bolshevik party, under Lenin, seized power from the moderate provisional government. As ardent socialists, the Bolsheviks accounted the war a capitalist plot, which they had no reason to continue. To justify their withdrawal, and to embarrass the capitalists, the Bolsheviks published various secret treaties by which the Allies agreed to split the spoils of victory.

Wilson had known of the existence of such treaties, if not of their details. But their airing compelled him to maintain America's distance from Britain and France, and encouraged him to spell out America's war aims more clearly than before. On January 8, 1918, he once again addressed Congress. "The day of conquest and aggrandizement is gone," he declared. "So is also the day of secret covenants entered into in the interest of particular governments and likely at some unlooked-for moment to upset the peace of the world." To make the purposes of the United States as transparent as possible, he outlined America's program of peace, which he also called "the program of the world's peace . . . the only possible program." It came in fourteen parts. First, "open covenants openly arrived at." No more secret treaties. Second, "absolute freedom of navigation upon the seas . . . alike in peace and war." Third, dismantling of barriers to trade among nations. Fourth, reductions in weapons of war. Fifth, adjustment of colonial claims, taking into account the wishes of the people ruled. Sixth through thirteenth, territorial settlements for Europe and the Ottoman Empire, based on similar considerations of equity and autonomy. Fourteenth and finally, establishment of "a general association of nations formed under specific covenants for the purpose of affording mutual guarantees of political independence and territorial integrity to great and small states alike."[23]

Wilson acknowledged that detail like this was unusual so far ahead of a peace conference. But considering the stakes of the war, and the challenge posed by the latest turn of events in Russia, it was appropriate—indeed, essential. "We have spoken now, surely, in terms too concrete to admit of any further doubt or question," he said. Beneath the specifics lay a single general principle. "It is the principle of justice to all peoples and nationalities, and their right to live on equal terms of liberty and safety with one another, whether they be strong or weak." On no other principle could lasting peace be founded, and on no other principle would the American people act. "To the vindication of this principle they are ready to devote their lives, their honor, and everything they possess. The moral climax of this, the culminating and final war for human liberty, has come, and they are ready to put their own strength, their own highest purpose, their own integrity and devotion to the test."[24]

Although Wilson's message was well received in the United States, foreign audiences were skeptical. French premier Georges Clemenceau was reported to have remarked that God gave men ten commandments and they broke every one; now Wilson wanted to impose fourteen. The British kept their doubts to themselves for the time being. The Germans answered emphatically—and brutally. In early March, in negotiations at Brest Litovsk, they imposed a victor's peace on Russia, a result that had the dual effect of freeing German troops for service on the western front and strongly suggesting that the larger war wouldn't end in any gentle Wilsonian peace, certainly not if Germany won.

Wilson felt obliged to respond, and he did so in language starkly different from any he had uttered till now. He said he had tried to determine whether the Germans sought justice or dominion in the present war. "They have answered, answered in unmistakable terms. They have avowed that it was not justice but dominion and the unhindered execution of their own will." Bad as this was for Russia, it was hardly better for America. Berlin's attitude meant that a German victory must be prevented at all costs, for it would mean an end to democracy and liberty wherever the German writ ran. "Everything that America has lived for and loved and grown great to vindicate and bring to a glorious resolution will have fallen in utter ruin and the gates of mercy once more piteously shut upon mankind!" Reason had given way to force, at least as far as Germany was concerned. "Germany has once more said that force, and force alone, shall decide whether justice and peace shall reign in the affairs of men, whether right as America conceives it or dominion as she conceives it shall determine the destinies of mankind. There is, therefore, but one response possible from us: force, force to the utmost, force without stint or limit, the righteous and triumphant force which shall make right the law of the world, and cast every selfish dominion down in the dust."[25]

Beyond stiffening his resolve toward Germany, the dictated peace of Brest Litovsk led Wilson into one of the more quixotic adventures in modern American foreign policy. The governments of Britain and France took the Bolshevik coup amiss on two accounts: once for the revolutionary virus Lenin and friends were setting loose upon the world, twice for dropping out of the war and making life on the western front that much harder. For both reasons London and Paris wanted to send troops to Russia: to stamp out the virus and to reopen the eastern front. And they wanted Washington to join them.

Wilson was no advocate of revolution, and he hardly relished the arrival of several hundred thousand additional German troops in France to fight America's doughboys. But neither did he want to be tarred with the brush of imperialism in a joint venture with the imperialists of Britain and France. For several months Wilson resisted British and French efforts to enlist the Americans in a landing in northern Russia. Meanwhile he kept a careful watch on Japan, which was preparing to invade Russian Siberia from the east. The Japanese didn't bother with ideological or strategic justifications; they simply hoped to grab some territory while the Russians were too weak to resist.

Wilson worried more about this issue than about almost anything else relating to the war. "I have been sweating blood over the question what it is right and feasible (*possible*) to do in

Russia," he wrote House. "It goes to pieces like quicksilver under my touch."[26]

An additional element slightly eased Wilson's dilemma. Since the closing of the eastern front a group of renegade Czechs—renegade from Austria-Hungary—had been trying to cross Russia to the Pacific, where they hoped to find transport to the western front in order to resume their struggle against the Central Powers. But amid the anarchy of Russia's revolution, they got stranded. Thereupon they appealed to Washington for rescue, cleverly casting themselves as freedom fighters in the tradition of the American patriots of 1776. The American public responded favorably, which mitigated the political risk to Wilson of intervention in Russia.

Ultimately the president consented to dispatch troops: five thousand to northern Russia and ten thousand to Siberia. In each case he did so less from agreement with the aims of his allies in intervention than from a desire to keep watch on those allies. Japan especially required watching, as its ambitions in northeast Asia had worried American officials since the late nineteenth century.

Both interventions proved a mess. By the time the British, French, and Americans reached northern Russia, there was no eastern front to reopen. The invaders became entangled in the Russian civil war—entangled enough to discredit the anti-Bolshevik forces but not enough to allow those forces to win. In Siberia, the Americans could merely watch as the Japanese invading force grew larger and larger. "The longer we stay, the more Japanese there are," reported War Secretary Baker.[27]

Both interventions long outlasted the war. American troops left northwestern Russia in the summer of 1919 and Siberia the following spring. They accomplished nothing good and left a legacy of distrust among the Russians, who never forgot—or allowed the West to forget—that the capitalists had tried to smother the socialist revolution in the cradle.

For several months after the American entry into the war, the flow of American soldiers across the Atlantic was scarcely more than a trickle. The troops had to be enlisted and trained, and the ships to transport them over the ocean had to be built or refitted. All this took time, and by the end of 1917 only 175,000 American soldiers had reached France.

During the spring of 1918, however, the trickle turned into a flood. By June 1918 their number had passed the 1 million mark and continued to increase at the rate of a quarter million per month.

It was a good thing the Americans got there when they did. Knowing the Americans were coming, the Germans threw all their troops and resources into a do-or-die offensive. They drove hard toward Paris and hurled British forces back toward the English Channel. For weeks the outcome hung in the balance— but with each passing week the balance shifted in favor of the Allies. Although the Americans took little active role in blunting the German offensive, their growing numbers allowed the British and French greater flexibility in meeting the German onslaught and at the same time dispirited the Germans.

By the time the Americans *did* engage the Germans seriously—at Château-Thierry and Belleau Wood in June, along the Marne in July—the worst was over. The German offensive had failed; the Allies would not lose. But whether they would win, and what they would win if they did, remained unanswered.

Wilson intended to supply much of that answer. After determining that the American Expeditionary Force would enter France as an independent fighting unit, the president left most of America's warmaking to General Pershing and his staff, but he kept full control of American peacemaking efforts. He decided, for example, that the United States would fight as an "Associated" power rather than an "Allied" power, the better to maintain his freedom of action in the diplomacy that would produce a postwar settlement. This didn't please the British and French, but it allowed Wilson to act as a broker between London and Paris, on one hand, and Berlin, on the other, in arranging an end to the fighting. He took as the basis for his brokering the Fourteen Points of January 1918.

Cool as they had been toward Wilson's points before, the British and French grew cooler as the war swung their way. With total Allied casualties in the millions, neither France's Clemenceau nor British prime minister David Lloyd George reckoned that he could ask voters to accept anything less than a resounding victory. They quibbled with one point or another of Wilson's fourteen—the British, having lived by the blockade, refused to accept unfettered freedom of the seas, while the French, whose invention of modern diplomacy was (and is still) evidenced by the predominance of French terms in diplomatic parlance, registered skepticism at the idea of open negotiations—but at bottom they were determined to dictate terms of peace to the Germans, not much differently than the Germans had dictated terms to the Russians.

By contrast, the Germans now saw merit in the Fourteen Points, even after Wilson elaborated on them in a September 27 speech that essentially asked the German people to overthrow their government. "We are all agreed that there can be no peace obtained by any kind of bargain or compromise with the governments of the Central Powers, because we have dealt with them already and have seen them deal with other governments that were parties to this struggle," he said. "They have convinced us that they are without honor and do not intend justice. They observe no covenants, accept no principle but force and their own interest. We cannot 'come to terms' with them. They have made it impossible. The German people must by this time be fully aware that we cannot accept the word of those who forced this war upon us."[28]

In the same speech, Wilson emphasized the essential righteousness of the American cause, speaking of it in transcendental language.

It has positive and well-defined purposes which we did not determine and which we cannot alter. No statesman or assembly created them; no statesman or assembly can alter them. . . . They were perhaps not clear at the outset; but they are clear now. The war has lasted more than four years, and the whole world has been drawn into it. The common will of mankind has been substituted for the particular purposes of individual states. Individual statesmen may have started the conflict, but neither they nor their opponents can stop it as they please. It has become a people's war, and peoples of all sorts and races, of every degree of power and variety of fortune, are involved in its sweeping processes of change and settlement. We came into it when its character had become fully defined and it was plain that no nation could stand apart or be indifferent to its outcome. Its challenge drove to the heart of every-thing we cared for and lived for. The voice of the war had become clear and gripped our hearts.[29]

Wilson didn't hesitate to speak in the voice of the war, on behalf of all those peoples swept up in the conflict. The central struggle, he said, was not over territory or reparations but over the fundamental issues of human intercourse.

Shall the military power of any nation or group of nations be suffered to determine the fortunes of peoples over whom they have no right to rule except the right to force? Shall strong nations be free to wrong weak nations and make them subject to their purpose and interest? Shall peoples be ruled and dominated, even in their own inter-nal affairs, by arbitrary and responsible force or by their own will and choice? Shall there be a common standard of right and privilege for all peoples and nations, or shall the strong do as they will and the weak suffer without redress? Shall the assertion of right be haphazard and by casual alliance, or shall there be a common concert to oblige the observance of common rights?[30]

It wouldn't have surprised Wilson to know that with this set of questions he essentially framed the core debate of interna-tional politics for the rest of the century; but at the moment he was content for his questions to point toward what he called the "indispensable instrumentality" of peace and justice, namely a "League of Nations." Without a League of Nations, any peace would rest, as heretofore throughout history, on the word of governments that were outlaws to one another—that is, on governments irresponsible to a higher authority. With a league, the world opinion the war had mobilized—"the common purpose of enlightened mankind"—would, by acting through this higher authority, restrain the strong, uphold the weak, and hearten the righteous. It was too early to specify details of the league but not too early to declare that the establishment of the league was "the most essential part of the peace settlement." And not too early to say that "the United States is prepared to assume its full share of responsibility."[31]

In the first week of October, the German government sued for an armistice on the basis of Wilson's Fourteen Points and his recent speech. Although his call for a German revolution was troubling to Berlin, his terms were better than anything the British or French were likely to offer. Indeed, the British and French complained to House, then in Paris, that the Germans were trying to play the Americans off against the Allies. "Their attempts in this direction must be foiled," British foreign secretary Arthur Balfour told House, who recounted the conversation to Wilson.[32]

Wilson wasn't about to let the Germans off the hook, but neither was he willing to indulge the desire of Britain and France for a harsh, vengeful peace, which, he believed, would simply render another war inevitable. Working through House, he coaxed and cajoled the British and French governments; when they persisted in their opposition to an end to the fighting, he directed House to threaten them with a separate German-American peace. "My statement had a very exciting effect on those present," House reported.[33]

Exciting enough that they acquiesced in Wilson's offer of the Fourteen Points as the basis for an armistice, subject to some minor reservations—or what they and Wilson were willing at this late hour to deem minor. Arranging the technical terms of the truce—when the shooting would stop, and how to ensure that the Germans didn't use the respite to regroup—required several days. It also required Wilson to overrule Pershing, who wanted to push on to the unconditional surrender of Germany.

On November 11, 1918, the armistice took effect. "A supreme moment of history has come," Wilson said in a statement issued from the White House. "The eyes of the people have been opened and they see. The hand of God is laid upon the nations. He will show them favor, I devoutly believe, only if they rise to the clear heights of His own justice and mercy."[34]

Later that day he addressed a joint session of Congress. After delineating the terms of the armistice, he summarized America's—and the world's—accomplishment. "The object of the war is attained: the object upon which all free men had set their hearts; and attained with a sweeping completeness which even now we do not realize." The armed imperialism of Germany had been thwarted, its evil designs frustrated. "And more than that— much more—has been accomplished. The great nations which associated themselves to destroy it have now definitely united in the common purpose to set up such a peace as will satisfy the longing of the whole world for disinterested justice, embodied in settlements which are based upon something much better and much more lasting than the selfish competitive interests of powerful states."[35]

# 4

## What We Dreamed at Our Birth

Yet there was a cloud over Wilson's triumph. The week before
the armistice, American voters had delivered control of Congress to the Republican party. Unsurprising in the context of
American political history, where voters' sixth-year itch has
often afflicted second-term presidents, the outcome was a blow
to Wilson, who had tried to make the congressional contests a
referendum on his handling of the war.

The attempt was a gamble, and a bad one. The Republicans
were still bitter at their hairbreadth defeat of 1916, and they
concluded that their losing margin was the result of their
unwillingness to distinguish themselves from Wilson on the war,
which at that time had remained a European contest. When
Wilson, having won on a platform of keeping America out of the
war, began his second term by taking America into the war, the
Republicans felt not only bitter but betrayed—or outsmarted,
which was worse. For the next two years they battled the
administration on nearly every aspect of the war. They waxed
indignant at what they considered Wilson's lack of vigor in pros-
ecuting the war; then, when he adopted measures to energize
the war effort, they condemned him for "socialistic tendencies."

Theodore Roosevelt missed no opportunity to castigate Wilson's war aims as hopelessly woolly. The League of Nations, Roosevelt declared, was a formula for German revival and American demoralization. "We intend to do justice to all other nations," Roosevelt said. "But in the last four years the professional internationalists, like the profound pacifists, have played the game of brutal German autocracy." In another speech, Roosevelt added, "To substitute internationalism for nationalism means to do away with patriotism. The professional pacifist and the professional internationalist are alike undesirable citizens."[1]

Nor could Wilson rely on the liberals. His winning coalition of 1916 had included many socialists and others on the left who considered him preferable to Hughes and the party of business. But since American entry into the war, the left had largely been silenced by the Sedition and Espionage acts. Recently even distribution of the venerable *Nation* had been halted on account of an editorial criticizing the administration for suppressing criticism. Wilson had no direct role in the action, and he moved quickly to overturn the order. But it seemed symptomatic of the administration's rightward drift, and it profoundly discouraged many of those who had looked to Wilson for leadership. Herbert Croly of the *New Republic* complained to Wilson that the repression was "dividing the body of public opinion into two irreconcilable classes" at a time when unity was required. Longtime progressive Amos Pinchot stated the matter more succinctly when he said of the president, "He puts his enemies in office and his friends in jail."[2]

Wilson was painfully aware of the criticism, which was why he judged a direct appeal to the voters in the autumn of 1918 necessary. "I believe it essential to the maintenance of my prestige abroad that we should re-elect a Democratic Congress," he told an associate.[3] Yet the mixing of patriotism and politics was a touchy business, and Wilson's closest advisers worried what it would bring. House, in Paris, accounted himself "gravely disturbed" at the idea. Edith Wilson, reading a draft of Wilson's message, told her husband bluntly, "I would not send it out. It is not a dignified thing to do."[4]

Yet Wilson insisted. He acknowledged that, from the standpoint of American politics, for a president of one party to have to deal with a Congress controlled by the other party would be nothing unheard of. "But the peoples of our Allies would never understand the matter," he said. "They would say that I had been repudiated." He related two incidents by way of explaining how the people of Europe were depending on him. He had learned that a girls' school in France had been used to barrack soldiers. The displaced girls were patriotic but wanted permission to play on the school grounds. The prefect refused, whereupon the girls protested: "Unless you allow us to do so, we shall take the case up with President Wilson, who is the final court of justice for the women of the world." The second incident involved longshoremen in Liverpool who were on strike for better hours and pay. They refused all appeals to go back to work—until the harbormaster shamed them by saying, "I want to ask you what President Wilson will think of you when he hears what your attitude is."[5]

So Wilson went ahead. "My fellow countrymen," he explained, "the Congressional elections are at hand. They occur in the most critical period our country has ever faced or is likely to face in our time. If you have approved of my leadership and wish me to continue to be your unembarrassed spokesman in affairs at home and abroad, I earnestly beg that you will express yourselves unmistakably to that effect by returning a Democratic majority to both the Senate and the House of Representatives." Had he stopped there, he might not have done himself too much damage. Presidents always campaign for their parties in off-year elections. But he went on to charge the Republicans with deliberately obstructing the administration's war efforts. "At almost every turn, since we entered the war, they have sought to take the choice of policy and the conduct of the war out of my hands and put it under the control of instrumentalities of their own choosing." And he detailed the likely consequences of voters' failure to heed his advice. "My power to administer the great trust assigned me by the Constitution would be seriously impaired should your judgment be adverse. . . . The return of a Republican majority to either House of the Congress would, moreover, certainly be interpreted on the other side of the water as a repudiation of my leadership."[6]

The Republicans cried foul. "A more ungracious, more unjust, more wanton, more mendacious accusation never was made by the most reckless stump orator, much less by a President of the United States," asserted Will Hays, the Republican national chairman.[7] And when voters—for reasons that had more to do with six years of accumulated small grievances than with any strong feeling on the war and the approaching peace—gave the Republicans control of not one but both houses of Congress, the GOP leadership held Wilson to his word. The president had been repudiated, they said, and they began to act accordingly. Theodore Roosevelt took the extraordinary step of writing to Clemenceau and British foreign secretary Balfour, pointing out that in a parliamentary system, the Democrats' defeat would have turned Wilson out of office. "He demanded a vote of confidence. The people voted a want of confidence," Roosevelt said.

He added significantly that the Republicans stood for "the unconditional surrender of Germany and for absolute loyalty to France and England in the peace negotiations."[8]

Wilson stirred up another controversy by deciding to attend the postwar peace conference himself. No other American president had ever done anything like this, and no other head of state would be there. Again Wilson's advisers questioned the wisdom of his decision. Secretary of State Lansing said it was a mistake. Journalist Frank Cobb, a longtime supporter and sounding board, wrote from Paris, "The moment the President sits at the council table with these Prime Ministers and Foreign Secretaries, he has lost all the power that comes from distance and detachment. Instead of remaining the great arbiter of human freedom he becomes merely a negotiator dealing with other negotiators. He is simply one vote in a Peace Conference that is bound either to abide by the will of the majority or disrupt its proceedings under circumstances which, having come to a climax in secret, can never be clearly explained to the public."[9]

But again Wilson overruled the naysayers. He wasn't simply a head of state; he was also a head of government, and in this regard quite the equivalent of Clemenceau and Lloyd George. Moreover, supremely confident of his eloquence, he knew that no one—not Lansing, not House—could speak as forcefully as he for the League of Nations, the linchpin, as he now saw it, of any satisfactory settlement.

He left New York on the morning of December 4, 1918. To judge by his send-off, the American people were enthusiastically behind him. Confetti rained down from the office windows of Manhattan as the president's entourage passed; horns, whistles, and sirens blared in the harbor as the *George Washington* slipped its mooring; airplanes and zeppelins circled overhead as the vessel cleared the Statue of Liberty.

The president's European arrival was even more enthusiastic. At Brest he was greeted with banners reading "Hail the Champion of the Rights of Man" and "Honor to the Founder of the Society of Nations." In Paris 2 million men, women, and children turned out to welcome "Wilson the Just." Front-row places along the route sold for three hundred francs; three divisions of French soldiers were required to keep the crowds from mobbing the American hero. As cannons boomed, Wilson's carriage nearly disappeared under hurled flowers. "I saw Foch pass, Clemenceau pass, Lloyd George, generals, returning troops," an American journalist remarked. "But Wilson heard from his carriage something different, inhuman—or superhuman."[10]

The adulation spread. Wilson journeyed to England and then to Italy, and everywhere met much the same response. Rome sprinkled its streets with golden sand, as per ancient tradition, and offered "Welcome to the God of Peace." Not even Caesar, the Romans said, had won a greater triumph from the people of the Eternal City. In Milan the crowds turned nearly hysterical; papers called him "The Savior of Humanity" and "The Moses from Across the Atlantic."[11]

In his addresses in America, Wilson had often claimed to speak for the peoples of the world; this uproarious reception confirmed his conviction that he was the tribune of humanity. "I do not believe that it was fancy on my part that I heard in the voice of welcome uttered in the streets of this great city and in the streets of Paris something more than a personal welcome," he told the lord mayor of London and a crowd at the Guildhall. "It seemed to me that I heard the voice of one people speaking to another people." What they were saying was what the soldiers Wilson had met were saying, although neither people nor soldiers had initially realized just what their words implied. It became clear—to Wilson, anyway—in talking with the troops. "As I have conversed with the soldiers, I have been more and more aware that they fought for something that not all of them had defined, but which all of them recognized the moment you stated it to them. They fought to do away with an old order and to establish a new one." The old order was based on the balance of power—that is, on fear, on force, on jealous self-interest and endless antagonism. The new order would be different, based on cooperation. It would be "a single overwhelming, powerful group of nations who shall be the trustee of the peace of the world." The American president was pleased to say that the Allied leaders with whom he had spoken shared his view—and therefore shared the view of the people of the world. "No such sudden and potent union of purpose has ever been witnessed in the world before."[12]

Wilson may not have been quite as convinced of the unity of purpose of the delegations as he let on; his remarks, which he essentially repeated in Paris and Rome, were as much exhortation as description. He had plenty to exhort about. The peace conference opened on January 12, and though the representatives of the victorious powers strove to present a united front to a curious world, fundamental divergences soon emerged. The British were more interested in preserving—and extending—their empire than in creating a League of Nations. The French placed priority on extracting reparations from Germany and taking other measures to ensure that their eastern neighbor would never trouble their sleep again.

As a result, Wilson was left to fight for the league more or less on his own. He succeeded in getting the league placed at the top of the agenda of the conference, and he headed the commission the conference appointed to draft a charter for the world body. From late January through mid-February he coaxed and cajoled the other members of the commission; on February 14 he was pleased to present the commission's handiwork to the conference.

The draft charter contained twenty-six articles, of which the one that drew the most attention was the tenth. "The High Contracting Parties undertake to respect and preserve as against external aggression the territorial integrity and existing political independence of all States members of the League," Wilson read to the assembled delegates. For Wilson, this was the heart of the league, and the heart of the work of the conference. What Wilson proposed was a guarantee of collective security: that an attack against one league member would be judged an attack against all and would be treated accordingly. No longer would world peace depend on the ability of states separately to deter or fend off attack; the league, acting as an international police force collectively more powerful than the strongest single nation, would deter aggression or, if deterrence failed, deliver exemplary punishment.[13]

Wilson didn't claim that the league charter as drafted was either perfect or definitive, which was why it allowed for amendment. "I should say of this document that it is not a straitjacket but a vehicle of life." Yet the basic principle embodied in Article Ten—of collective responsibility for world peace—must abide. "While it is elastic, while it is general in its terms, it is definite in the one thing that we were called upon to make definite. It is a definite guarantee of peace. . . . It is a definite guarantee against the things which have just come near bringing the whole structure of civilization into ruin. Its purposes do not for a moment lie vague. Its purposes are declared and its powers made unmistakable."[14]

Shortly thereafter Wilson boarded the *George Washington* and sailed for home. The conference wasn't over, and he made clear he would be back. But no American president had ever been gone from the United States so long, and with the Republicans newly in control of Congress, Wilson felt obliged to return to Washington to remind them that the Democrats still ran the executive branch. At the same time, his departure at just this moment, with the league newly born, was also an exercise in symbolism. It was the league for which he had come to Paris; lesser matters he could entrust to his subordinates.

Between Wilson's December departure from America and his February return, his foremost political antagonist died. Theodore Roosevelt succumbed in his sleep in January 1919 (causing one observer to remark that death had to take him sleeping since it never could have conquered him awake). Roosevelt's death removed the most prominent threat to Wilson's hopes for a League of Nations, but others remained. Of these, the one that emerged as the most dangerous was Henry Cabot Lodge of Massachusetts, a longtime ally of Roosevelt.

Lodge disliked Wilson on grounds both personal and political. Until Wilson came along, Lodge, with three Harvard degrees and a Harvard professorship before being elected to the House of Representatives and then the Senate, had relished his reputation as the nation's "scholar in politics." Wilson eclipsed Lodge on both counts, proving a better scholar and a more successful politician. As a partisan Republican, Lodge instinctively resisted most of what the Democratic president proposed, and he was loath to yield anything that might be used against the GOP in the 1920 elections. As an American nationalist, he rejected Wilson's internationalist vision of collective security via a League of Nations, preferring that America deal with America's problems in America's own way. As a foreign-policy pragmatist, he scorned what he considered Wilson's naive idealism, complaining that it showed a dearth of experience of the world beyond the ivory tower. And as chairman of the Senate Foreign Relations Committee, Lodge was strategically placed to make Wilson's life miserable regarding any treaty that might emerge from Paris.

Wilson understood what he faced in Lodge, and he accepted the challenge. Directing the captain of the *George Washington* to land at Boston, the president commenced his American campaign for the league in Lodge's own backyard. Wilson declined to mention Lodge by name, but few listeners missed his reference when he recounted an interview he had had in Paris with a group of visiting scholars. "I told them that I had had one of the delightful revenges that sometimes come to men. All my life I have heard men speak with a sort of condescension of ideals and of idealists, and particularly of those separated, encloistered persons whom they choose to term academic, who were in the habit of uttering ideals in a free atmosphere when they clash with nobody in particular. And I said I have had this sweet revenge. Speaking with perfect frankness in the name of the people of the United States, I have uttered as the objects of this war great ideals, and nothing but ideals. And the war has been won by that inspiration." Again avoiding Lodge's name, Wilson warned him and all others who stood against the league and the ideals it embodied: "Any man who resists the present tides that run in the world will find himself thrown upon a shore so high and barren that it will seem as if he had been separated from his human kind forever."[15]

Wilson kept up the pressure after he reached Washington. Speaking to the Democratic National Committee, he lashed the opponents of the league in the harshest terms. "Of all the blind and little provincial people, they are the littlest and most contemptible," he declared. "They remind me of a man with a head that is not a head but is just a knot providentially put there to keep him from raveling out. But why the Lord should not have been willing to let them ravel out, I do not know. . . . The whole impulse of the modern time is against them. They are going to have the most conspicuously contemptible names in history. The gibbets that they are going to be erected on by future historians will scrape the heavens, they will be so high." The saving grace of the situation was that these small minds and shriveled souls were a distinct minority. The American people knew right and wisdom from wrong and folly, and the American people would prevail. Yet the president wished for the victory to come soon. "I am not concerned as to the ultimate outcome of this thing at all, not for a moment, but I am concerned that the outcome should be brought about immediately, just as promptly as possible. So my hope is that we will all put on our war paint, not as Democrats but as Americans, get the true American pattern of war paint and a real hatchet and go out on the war path and get a collection of scalps that has never been excelled in the history of American warfare."[16]

Lodge struck back. Although he was canny enough not to denounce a treaty that had yet to be written, he made clear that the Senate would scrutinize with the utmost care anything Wilson brought home from Paris. And the burden of proof would be on the president to prove that the treaty preserved the cardinal tenets of American foreign policy: the Monroe Doctrine, nonentanglement in the affairs of other countries, and especially American sovereignty in matters of war and peace. As further warning, Lodge introduced an antileague resolution signed by enough Republicans to block any treaty containing such an international organization. And as a token of their power, Lodge and the rest of the Republican leadership stalled legislation until after Wilson's departure for Paris. Wilson's stated reason for coming home had been to sign laws and deal with other matters that required the president's personal attention; the Republicans pointedly ensured that he had wasted his time.

Wilson delivered his rejoinder just before embarking again for France. To show that Lodge didn't speak for all Republicans, Wilson linked arms with former president Taft at a bipartisan rally in favor of the League of Nations at New York's Metropolitan Opera House. "The first thing I am going to tell the people on the other side of the water is that an overwhelming majority of the American people is in favor of the League of Nations," Wilson said. (In those days before scientific polling, Wilson had no way of proving that this was true, but neither did his opponents have any way of proving it wasn't.) He conceded that a vocal minority opposed the league. "I do not know by what influences they have been blinded"—actually he thought he did know, but in the present forum he preferred not to cite personal jealousy and partisan ambition—"but I do know they have been separated from the general currents of the thought of mankind. And I want to utter this solemn warning, not in the way of a threat; the forces of the world do not threaten, they operate. The great tides of the world do not give notice that they are going to rise and run; they rise in their majesty and overwhelming might, and those who stand in the way are overwhelmed." Switching metaphors, the president asserted, "The heart of the world is awake, and the heart of the world must be satisfied. . . . Men have at last perceived that the only permanent thing in the world is the right, and that a wrong settlement is bound to be a temporary settlement." He told how he had spoken to wounded soldiers in Europe, who implored him to prevent future generations from having to make the sacrifices they had made. "It is inconceivable that we should disappoint them, and we shall not."[17]

Upon Wilson's return to Paris, the inconceivable became all too conceivable. Clemenceau and Lloyd George had taken advantage of Wilson's absence to solidify their own positions, and they did so with the cooperation of Edward House. Previously content to operate unofficially, House had lately accepted a formal appointment as a delegate to the conference and, in Wilson's absence, he acted as the president's proxy. The authority went to his head, and he cut deals with the British and French that Wilson would never have countenanced in person. Nothing was final, of course, till Wilson approved it, and in fact he did disown certain of House's innovations. But he couldn't disown them all without admitting he didn't control his delegation, an admission that would have weakened him with the other chiefs present. Wilson's embarrassment became anger at House, and the contretemps marked the beginning of the end of the productive relationship between the two. A parting had probably been inevitable since Wilson's marriage to Edith, who treated all Wilson's advisers with distrust; the strain of the peace conference simply precipitated it. Anyway, as telling as Wilson's embarrassment was the fact that House's sympathy for the British and French provided Lloyd George and Clemenceau evidence, beyond that afforded by the disastrous congressional elections of the previous autumn, that Wilson was negotiating not from strength among his own people but from hope—a circumstance that caused Wilson, with Edith's encouragement, to blame House the more.

Wilson's weakness became evident during the second half of the peace conference. Lloyd George was on record with talk of hanging the kaiser and squeezing the German lemon "till the pips squeak," and as the conference shifted from the speech-making phase to the treaty-writing phase, he increasingly insisted on German accountability and reparations, in addition to pro-tection for Britain's empire. Clemenceau had been the victim of an assassination attempt during Wilson's absence; the serious wounds he received hardened his determination to finish the war's work by putting French security forever beyond the reach of German aggression. With Lloyd George he demanded repara-tions; he also insisted on French control of large parts of Ger-many's most productive territory.

Transcending the details of Germany's treatment, a basic philosophical difference separated Wilson from his European counterparts (not unlike that which separated Wilson from Lodge and his other opponents at home). Wilson remained a progressive, and as such an optimist regarding human nature. The crimes of humanity—crimes including the war just ended—he ascribed to bad leadership and maladaptive institutions, not to any intrinsic human penchant for evil. A rightly written treaty, including a League of Nations, would allow the better angels of men to rise above the evils of the past. Clemenceau and Lloyd George had once shared this optimism, but political maturity and especially the war disabused them of it. (Informed that his son had joined the Communist party, Clemenceau reportedly replied, "My son is twenty-two years old. If he had not become a Communist at twenty-two, I would have dis-owned him. If he is still a Communist at thirty, I will do it then.")[18] Having witnessed the worst of human nature, and at much closer hand than Wilson had, the Europeans expected the worst. Where the idealistic Wilson hoped to liberate the angels in men, the realistic Lloyd George and Clemenceau were content to chain men's devils.

Remarks that passed between Wilson and Clemenceau revealed the philosophical gap between the American leader and his British and French counterparts. Clemenceau was demanding French control of the coal-rich Saar region of Germany; Wilson was resisting.[19] "If we do not wish to place ourselves in the wrong and break our word," Wilson said, "we must not interpret our own principles too generously to our benefit. I say this solemnly: Let us avoid acting in a manner which would risk creating sympathies for Germany; neither let us seek to interpret our promises with a lawyer's finesse."

"I will keep in mind the words and excellent intentions of President Wilson," Clemenceau answered. But the French leader demurred nonetheless. Speaking of Wilson, to Wilson, he said, "He eliminates sentiment and memory." Clemenceau continued: "It is there that I have a reservation about what has just been said. The President of the United States disregards the depths of human nature. The fact of the war cannot be forgotten. America did not see this war at a close distance for its first three years; during this time we lost a million and a half men. . . . You seek to do justice to the Germans. Do not believe that they will ever forgive us; they only seek the opportunity for revenge. Nothing will destroy the rage of those who wanted to establish their domination over the world and who believed themselves so close to succeeding."

Wilson stuck by his principles and wanted to ensure that Clemenceau did, too. "What I seek is not to deviate from the path being followed by this great world movement toward justice," he explained. "I wish to do nothing which would allow it to be said of us: 'They profess great principles, but they admitted exceptions everywhere, wherever sentiment or national interest made them wish to deviate from the rule.'"

The exchange escalated. Clemenceau accused Wilson of being pro-German.

"In that event," Wilson responded, "do you wish me to return home?"

"I do not wish you to go home," Clemenceau declared. "But I intend to do so myself." And he stalked out of the session.

Complicating Wilson's task further were the expectations of various Americans regarding the league. In February, Taft and other friends of the league had convinced the president that certain amendments to the proposed charter were necessary for Senate approval. Americans who knew history recalled how troublesome the first American alliance, with France during the American Revolution, had become after the outbreak of France's own revolution, and demanded an escape clause. Others, of fretful disposition, feared that the league would meddle in American domestic affairs, and wanted an explicit exclusion of home issues from the league's consideration. Still others, particularly proud of America's earliest statement of hemispheric purpose, craved assurance that the league wouldn't infringe on the Monroe Doctrine.

Though often accounted unbending, Wilson showed remarkable flexibility on these points. He inserted an escape clause into the league charter, despite thinking it superfluous. He accepted an amendment exempting domestic issues from the league's purview, despite thinking it silly. He carved a special status for the Monroe Doctrine, despite thinking it invidious.

Meanwhile he fought a rearguard action against the nationalist demands of Lloyd George and Clemenceau, despite grave concerns at where those demands were leading. (Less serious were the demands of Italian prime minister Vittorio Orlando, the last member of the so-called Big Four at the conference. When Orlando laid claim to the Adriatic port of Fiume on grounds that the language, population, and culture of the city were overwhelmingly Italian, Wilson put him off with a joke: "I hope you won't press that point with respect to New York City, or you might feel like claiming a sizable piece of Manhattan Island."[20] Orlando was not amused.) Lloyd George and Clemenceau, as leaders of the two great European empires, resisted and resented Wilson's call for self-determination for subject peoples. They could accept the idea of self-determination as applied to the German, Austrian, and Ottoman empires, some of whose pieces they expected to snatch up (in defiance—allegedly temporary—of the very principle of self-determination). But they had no intention of allowing the notion to intrude upon their own empires. Wilson couldn't change their minds. Yet the American president's endorsement of self-determination, even if only in principle, gave the concept a credibility it couldn't have gained otherwise—and planted a time bomb beneath the British and French empires that would explode a generation hence.

The last weeks of the conference were rocky. At one stage Wilson threatened again to leave and went so far as to order the captain of the *George Washington* to ready the vessel for immediate departure. But he didn't follow through, judging that an imperfect peace was better than none. Partly to console others, who had taken him at his idealistic word, and partly to soothe himself, Wilson explained, "You cannot throw off the habits of society immediately any more than you can throw off the habits of the individual immediately. They must be slowly got rid of, or, rather, they must be slowly altered." Waxing metaphoric, he said, "You cannot in human experience rush into the light. You have to go through the twilight into the broadening day before the noon comes and the full sun is upon the landscape."[21]

The quid pro quo for Wilson's compromises was acceptance by the British and French of the League of Nations. In the final version of the treaty, signed on June 28 in the Hall of Mirrors of the palace at Versailles, Lloyd George got his pips, in the form of a huge reparations bill against Germany (which would pay France as well). Clemenceau got control of the Saar and other security guarantees. Wilson got his league.

Or, rather, he would get his league if he could deliver the Senate. This was no sure thing, given the hostility already evinced by Lodge and his fellow Republicans. Wilson's compromises at Paris had mollified certain critics of the league, but a wall of opposition remained. Its left flank comprised liberals who believed that Wilson had surrendered too much at Paris, that the treaty was an unholy bargain with those reactionary devils Lloyd George and Clemenceau. This part of the opposition was essentially passive, consisting of former political allies who might have backed Wilson on the treaty but now didn't. The right flank of the wall was higher, stronger, and more actively defended; its ramparts were manned by conservatives who looked askance at anything that might diminish America's freedom of action—in particular, the League of Nations and its insidious Article Ten. Wilson's task during the summer of 1919 was to find, or create, enough space between the disillusioned liberals and the adamant conserva-

tives to boost the treaty over the center of the wall, where—
he hoped—two-thirds of the Senate might be found.

He looked for help among the American people, and he
relied in the search on his powers of persuasion. It might have
seemed to Wilson that this was the task for which he had been
preparing his whole life. Against the parliamentary wiles of
Lodge and the numerical advantage of the Republicans, and the
sullen apathy of the liberals, Wilson had only his way with
words. He was a lame duck; he couldn't credibly threaten the
senators. He could only appeal to the American people, create
a groundswell of support for the league and the idealism it
embodied, and by this means force the Senate to do the right
thing. It was a task worthy of the great orators he had studied; it
was a task worthy of the great orator he always wanted to be.

His campaign commenced before he left France. On the
American Memorial Day he visited American graves at the
Suresnes Cemetery. "No one with a heart in his breast, no American, no lover of humanity, can stand in the presence of these
graves without the most profound emotion," he said. "Never
before have men crossed the seas to a foreign land to fight for
a cause which they did not pretend was peculiarly their own,
but knew was the cause of humanity and of mankind." The living could honor the dead—the living *must* honor the dead—by
completing the task for which these brave men had given their
lives. "These men did not come across the sea merely to defeat
Germany and her associated powers in the war. They came to
defeat forever the things for which the Central Powers stood, the
sort of power they meant to assert in the world, the arrogant,
selfish dominance which they meant to establish; and they came,
moreover, to see to it that there should never be a war like this

again." They had fallen, but others picked up the torch—yet not without a struggle. "There is here and there an attempt to insert into the counsel of statesmen the old reckonings of selfishness and bargaining and national advantage which were the roots of this war." Those, however, who adopted this shortsighted view would fail. "The peoples of the world are awake, and the peoples of the world are in the saddle. Private counsels of statesmen cannot now and cannot hereafter determine the destinies of nations. . . . This is an age which looks forward, not backward; which rejects the standards of national selfishness that once governed the counsels of nations and demands that they shall give way to a new order of things in which the only questions will be: 'Is it right?' 'Is it just?' 'Is it in the interest of mankind?' ' "[22]

Wilson's campaign for the league continued upon his arrival in America. Some of his advisers urged him to adopt a conciliatory stance toward the skeptics of the treaty. House urged him to seek common ground; if he showed the senators the same consideration he had shown Lloyd George and Clemenceau, House said, all would be well. Wilson replied that the time for conciliation was past. "I have found that one can never get anything in this life that is worthwhile without fighting for it," he declared.[23]

On July 10 Wilson personally delivered the treaty to the Senate (breaking another long-standing tradition). Despite a torrential rain that day, the gallery of the upper chamber was jammed with onlookers eager to see the president take on his opponents. Lodge escorted Wilson in. "Mr. President," he said, "can I carry the treaty for you?" "Not on your life," Wilson responded.[24]

As he physically laid the treaty out for inspection, Wilson summarized what it contained—and what it meant. He reminded his listeners that the United States had entered the war upon a different basis than had the other opponents of Germany. "We entered it, not because our material interests were directly threatened or because any special treaty obligations to which we were parties had been violated, but only because we saw the supremacy, and even the validity, of right everywhere put in jeopardy and free government everywhere imperiled. . . . We entered the war as the disinterested champions of right." Lodge and some of the senators might have objected here, recalling that the sinking of American ships was what had prompted *them* to vote for war. But this was Wilson's moment, and they kept still. The president asserted the United States had negotiated the peace in the same way it had fought the war, as the disinterested champion of right. And America must remain the champion of right. "There can be no question of our ceasing to be a world power. The only question is whether we can refuse the moral leadership that is offered us, whether we shall accept or reject the confidence of the world." Wilson's peroration must have stirred even those it didn't convince.

The stage is set, the destiny disclosed. It has come about by no plan of our conceiving, but by the hand of God who led us into this way. We cannot turn back. We can only go forward, with lifted eyes and freshened spirit, to follow the vision. It was of this that we dreamed at our birth. America shall in truth show the way. The light streams upon the path ahead, and nowhere else.[25]

Lodge knew he couldn't match Wilson's eloquence, and he didn't try. Instead he employed a strategy of delay and sapping. He read the entire treaty, word by word, slowly and aloud, killing two weeks. He held hearings whose purpose was less to enlighten than to take more time, on the premise that the enthusiasm for the treaty must diminish as America's attention turned from the peace conference lately concluded to the affairs of ordinary life now resumed. He entertained amendments to the treaty by the dozens, then the scores—some reasonable, some transparently obstructive.

Wilson countered by opening the doors of the White House to the senators, inviting them to drop by any morning with questions or comments. He held more formal sessions with groups of senators, including one full morning with Lodge and the Foreign Relations Committee. In these meetings he made clear that he could accept the idea of interpretive reservations to the treaty: statements by the Senate of its understanding of particular clauses and articles. But he could not accept substantive amendments to the treaty itself. Amendments would require the approval of the other parties to the treaty; recalling how difficult the closing phases of the Paris conference had been, the president feared that any resumption of negotiations would cause the entire treaty to unravel.

Wilson had hoped for a quick vote on the treaty; when Lodge succeeded in stalling into September, with little prospect of a vote before October or November, the president decided to take his case to the people. Abandoning Washington, he headed west on a cross-country speaking tour on behalf of the treaty and the league. Had he held office a decade hence, he could have addressed the nation by radio; four decades hence, by television. But in 1919 the only way he could let America hear his voice was to visit America personally.

He kicked off the tour in Columbus, Ohio, where cold rain and a trolley strike diminished the turnout. In Indiana and Missouri the crowds were better, and despite the arrival of squads of Republicans dispatched to counter the president's message, Wilson's listeners responded enthusiastically. In St. Louis he explained what he would have to say to American veterans of the war if the Senate rejected the treaty: "You are betrayed. You fought for something that you did not get." Speaking more directly to his audience, Wilson continued:

And the glory of the armies and navies of the United States is gone like a dream in the night, and there ensues upon it, in the suitable darkness of the night, the nightmare of dread which lay upon the nations before this war came. And there will come some time, in the vengeful Providence of God, another struggle in which not a few hundred thousand fine men from America will have to die, but as many millions as are necessary to accomplish the final freedom of the peoples of the world.[26]

In Montana and Idaho—the latter the home of arch-isolationist Senator William Borah—Wilson's reception was somewhat cooler, but on the Pacific coast he again struck a favorable chord. "The spirit of the crowd seemed at times akin to fanaticism," observed a reporter for the *New York Times,* filing from Seattle. A few days later, the *Times* recapped the outbound leg of the president's tour: "It seems a safe assertion that the ten states through which he has passed believe with him that the Treaty of Peace should be ratified without delay and that they are willing to bring the United States into a League of Nations."[27]

Wilson's train swung south into California. In Sacramento he praised the charter covenant of the league as a landmark in human history. "The Covenant is a movement to make for the betterment of the world." Rejection of the treaty and the league would condemn the world to a grim fate. "Without this treaty, without the Covenant of the League of Nations which it contains, we would simply sink back into that slough of despond in which mankind was before this war began, with the strain of war and of terror constantly over them. We cannot go back. We will not go back."[28]

Wilson turned east. In Ogden, Utah, he claimed a mandate from the American people. "There is no sort of doubt that 80 per cent of the people of the United States are for the League of Nations," he said. As for that willful minority who opposed it, they kept bad company. "All the elements that tended toward disloyalty are against the League, and for a very good reason. If this League is not adopted, we will serve Germany's purpose."[29]

The stress of the tour on Wilson was very great; the president spoke for hours a day, for weeks on end. But at each stop he summoned the energy to move his audience with his vision of America's future, and the world's. At Pueblo, Colorado, he declared, "Now that the mists of this great question have cleared away, I believe that men will see the truth, eye to eye and face to face. There is one thing that the American people always rise to and extend their hand to, and that is the truth of justice and of liberty and of peace. We have accepted that truth, and we are going to be led by it, and it is going to lead us, and through us, the world, out into pastures of quietness and peace such as the world never dreamed of before."[30]

And with those words he suddenly fell silent.

For many years Wilson had experienced high blood pressure. This condition wasn't especially serious when his arteries were young and elastic, but with advancing age the risk to his health—especially his neurological health—increased. In 1896 he suffered a cerebral incident, probably a minor stroke, that cost him the use of his right hand temporarily. (The fact that he was quickly able to learn to write with his left hand suggests, in conjunction with his childhood tardiness in reading, that he may have been dyslexic.) In 1906 another apparent stroke, again minor, prompted a long holiday in Bermuda. In the same year, his hypertension burst a blood vessel in his left eye, rendering him briefly blind, and permanently visually impaired, on that side. In 1908 he again lost the use of his right hand, again temporarily.

As president, he took care to pace himself, to get sufficient rest and exercise, and for several years his hypertension appeared to be under control. But his efforts at the peace conference and in the fight for the league exacted a price. In April 1919 he experienced another cerebral incident. His doctor, Cary Grayson, denied that it was a stroke, telling Lloyd George and others that the president had simply caught the flu that was going around (the world) and that this exacerbated a long-standing nervous condition that produced a twitching of the face. Yet a neurologist summoned to examine the president concluded that the patient had suffered a "stroke so destructive as that it had made of him a changeling with a very different personality and a markedly lessened ability."[31] Others noticed the change as well. Ike Hoover, a veteran White House usher, said the president "was never the same" after this attack.[32] And even Grayson recorded a strange episode in which Wilson insisted on rearranging the furniture in his Paris apartment. "I don't like the way the colors of this furniture fight each other," the president said. "The greens and the reds are all mixed up here and there is no harmony. Here is a big purple, high-backed covered chair, which is like the Purple Cow, strayed off to itself, and it is placed where the light shines on it too brightly. If you will give me a lift, we will move this next to the wall where the light from the window will give it a subdued effect. And here are two chairs, one green and the other red. This will never do. Let's put the greens all together and the reds together."[33]

Yet, as after his earlier attacks, Wilson rebounded quickly. Some of his best work at the peace conference occurred in the months after the April incident, and he never spoke more eloquently in favor of the league. But the weariness of six years in office and six months of peacemaking was hard to shake. In July he experienced another incident, probably a small stroke. And beginning in late September, in the hours and days after his Pueblo speech, he suffered an attack that culminated in a major and incapacitating stroke.

The first symptoms surfaced just twenty miles from Pueblo. The president complained of severe discomfort and an inability to breathe. Grayson halted the train and took Wilson outside for a walk. The fresh air helped, and the president reboarded the train. Several miles farther on he managed to wave from the rear platform to a small crowd gathered to see him pass. As night fell he took to his berth, but he awoke before midnight, feeling acute pain, and had to sit up in bed to alleviate it, slightly. An audience awaited him at Wichita, Kansas, and he badly wanted to speak to them, to win that much more support for the league. But he couldn't get dressed, nor even get out of bed. Puzzled and pained, he told Joseph Tumulty, "I don't seem to realize it, but I seem to have gone to pieces." Grayson, who overheard the remark, added in his diary: "The President looked out of the window and he was almost overcome by his emotions. He choked and big tears fell from his eyes as he turned away."[34]

Things got worse. Tumulty and Grayson conferred with Edith, and the three determined that the rest of the trip must be canceled. With curtains drawn on the president's car and other traffic shunted aside, Wilson's train rolled straight through to Washington. He summoned sufficient strength to walk through Union Station, and for four days at the White House he appeared to be getting better. But on October 2 he collapsed on the floor of the bathroom, where Edith found him, bloody and unconscious. She and Grayson got him undressed and onto the Lincoln bed, where he lay stretched out and ghastly. "He looked as if he were dead," Ike Hoover recalled. "There was not a sign of life. His face had a long cut about the temple from which the signs of blood were still evident. His nose also bore a long cut lengthwise. This too looked red and raw."[35]

In fact he wasn't dead, but when he regained consciousness he and the others discovered that his left side was paralyzed. The cause of the paralysis (and of the fall) was another stroke, this far more serious and debilitating than any of the previous ones. Just *how* debilitating was a matter of great controversy then and since. Grayson, Tumulty, and especially Edith conspired to shield the public from full knowledge of the president's disability. Grayson, by word and mien, emphasized the positive. "The President had a very good night," he said on October 6. "His appetite is improving and he is sleeping better."[36] A reporter remarked: "Dr. Grayson continues to show by his demeanor that the President is improving. Tonight he was even more cheerful than after he left the forenoon conference."[37] When Robert Lansing inquired whether presidential authority ought to pass to Vice President Thomas Marshall, Grayson and Tumulty linked arms against the secretary of state. "While Woodrow Wilson is lying in the White House on the broad of his back I will not be a party to ousting him," Tumulty declared. "He has been too kind, too loyal, and too wonderful to me to receive such treatment at my hands." In his recounting of the moment, Tumulty added, "Just as I uttered this statement Doctor Grayson appeared in the Cabinet Room and I turned to him and said: 'And I am sure Doctor Grayson will never certify to his disability. Will you, Grayson?' Doctor Grayson left no doubt in Mr. Lansing's mind that he would not do as Mr. Lansing suggested."[38] Placing personal loyalty above public interest, Grayson and Tumulty issued a series of statements from the president's office that ascribed to nervous exhaustion and neurasthenia his failure to appear in public and otherwise perform his duties.

Behind the curtain took place a unique and astonishing chapter in the history of the American presidency. For seventeen months Edith, Grayson, and Tumulty kept the true state of Wilson's condition secret from the American people, and during most of that period Edith served as the sole conduit between the president and the rest of the world. She afterward acknowledged the extraordinary position she occupied: "I studied every paper, sent from the different Secretaries or Senators, and tried to digest and present in tabloid form the things that, despite my vigilance, had to go to the President. I, myself, never made a single decision regarding the disposition of public affairs. The only decision that was mine was what was important and what was not, and the *very* important decision of when to present matters to my husband."[39]

Whether Edith told the truth in disclaiming substantive decision making can't be known. She certainly didn't decide the large issues, such as whether to compromise on the league. But in any administration, the one who controls information strongly shapes decisions, and Edith definitely did that. She had no apparent agenda separate from her husband's, but she was exceedingly protective of his health, first, and his presidential prerogatives and reputation, second.

Those beyond the inner circle didn't know what to make of the situation. Even assuming Edith transmitted their messages and queries fully and honestly, they couldn't discern how much Wilson understood of what she brought him. Lansing thought it wasn't much. In November the secretary of state drafted a Thanksgiving proclamation for the president's signature and sent it through Edith. Two days later it came back with the president's seal and not a single addition or correction. Lansing judged himself a fair wordsmith, but the old Wilson had never missed an opportunity to improve on his subordinates' prose. Moreover, the president's signature, formerly bold and decisive, was now an ugly and nearly illegible scrawl.

In most administrations at most times, the American ship of state sails tolerably well with hands other than the president's at the helm. And so it sailed now, on most matters. Some appointments were slow, and many bills became law without the president's signature. Tumulty drafted a message vetoing the Volstead Act (the measure to enforce the Eighteenth Amendment, which established prohibition; Wilson thought the Volstead law unenforceable), but Congress, as expected, overrode the veto.

Yet certain matters required the president's personal attention, and by far the most pressing of these was the Versailles treaty. During Wilson's western tour and now during the president's illness, Lodge marshaled the opposition to the treaty. This opposition included a dozen Republican "irreconcilables," who were set against the league in any form, and the larger group of Republicans who wouldn't flatly oppose the treaty and the league but insisted on reservations. These reservations touched various aspects of the treaty, but the most important involved Article Ten of the league covenant, the kernel of the collective security idea. While the different senators described their concerns in various words, the gist of the worry was that the offending article amounted to a blank check on American blood and treasure, payable whenever some idiots overseas got themselves into a war.

At times during the autumn of 1919, it was impossible to tell whether the Republican reservations were an honest attempt to fix what was wrong with the treaty or a stalking horse for outright rejection. For some Republicans, including Lodge, they were both. Lodge was operating from strength against Wilson: both the strength of the Republican majority in the Senate and the strength of the constitutional requirement for a supermajority of two-thirds to ratify treaties. Given that Wilson lacked the votes for ratification without reservations, Lodge would win no matter what the president did. If Wilson accepted the reservations, the treaty (assuming it survived the rescrutiny of the other signers) would reflect the Republicans' insistence on America's freedom of action. If Wilson rejected the reservations, the treaty would go down to defeat.

The treaty's only hope was for some flexibility from Wilson, some willingness to accommodate the concerns of borderline reservationists. The Wilson of 1913 and 1914, the legislative strategist who co-opted Roosevelt's New Nationalist philosophy in the name of the New Freedom, almost certainly would have bent sufficiently. But the Wilson of 1919 couldn't manage the feat. Perhaps in his mental fog and his isolation from the world beyond his sickroom, he underestimated the opposition in the Senate and overestimated the popular support for the treaty. Perhaps his hardened arteries simply hardened his will. But whatever the cause, he resisted all pleas to meet Lodge halfway. Senator Gilbert Hitchcock, the Democratic minority leader, implored Wilson to compromise, arguing that a treaty with reservations was better than no treaty at all. Hitchcock wrote Wilson a letter urging the president to give his blessing to Senate Democrats who wanted to vote for a reserved treaty. He got no answer. He wrote again, and this time received a reply from Mrs. Wilson. The president, Edith declared, could not accept ratification with the proposed reservations.

Hitchcock, desperate to save the president from himself—or perhaps from his wife—demanded to see Wilson. Edith tried to stop him, but under the circumstances she couldn't flatly deny permission. The afternoon of the meeting was mild for November, and Edith had the president wheeled onto the south lawn of the White House. Hitchcock was startled by what he saw. "I beheld an emaciated old man with a thin white beard," he recalled. The president, obviously confused, brightened briefly when the senator explained that the Democrats were sticking together, but when Hitchcock listed those who could be counted on to vote for an unreserved treaty, and fell far short of the number required for approval, the president groaned, "Is it possible? Is it possible?"[40]

Yet nothing Hitchcock could say would change Wilson's mind. Between the reality of ratification politics and the idealism of his vision for the league, the president chose the latter and refused to release the Democrats. The Senate voted, and the treaty fell short by eight votes.

The president's friends—or, in many cases, former friends, now ostracized by Edith—found it increasingly difficult to sympathize with his predicament. Lansing fumed at the conspiracy that controlled the White House. "If it ever gets out it will make a fine scandal," the secretary of state said.[41] He resigned shortly thereafter.

Following the negative vote in the Senate, Wilson fantasized about engineering a kind of referendum on the treaty. He would challenge the senators who had voted against the treaty to resign their offices and submit to special elections. If a majority of them won, he would accept the judgment of the people and then resign his own office. Wiser heads derailed this particular scheme but not Wilson's desire to appeal again to the American people over the heads of the Senate. During the spring of 1920 he tried to commit the Democratic party to a presidential campaign cast as a referendum on the treaty and the league. For several months, he even fancied himself a candidate for a third term, despite the utter unrealism of the idea.

It was a tragic end to a presidency that had started with such promise. Senate Democrats, hoping to salvage something from the ruins, broke with Wilson on a second treaty vote and accepted Lodge's reservations; but even their backing failed to put the ratifiers past the requisite two-thirds mark. As it involved the United States, the treaty died, and with it Wilson's dream of American leadership in the new world beyond the war.

5

## Provincials No Longer

Woodrow Wilson lived too long and then died too soon. His
final years saw a reaction against the idealism that had drawn
him into politics and had served as his guide to American diplomacy. He was right to have worried about the war's effect on the
reforming spirit in America, for although the war left in place,
and indeed strengthened, the agencies of progressivism, it per-
verted much of their purpose. Implicit in progressivism had
always been the notion that people could be made better by
appropriate encouragement: better education, better working
conditions, better housing, better laws. During the war, the
encouragement often became coercive. The Espionage and Sedition acts were part of the coercion; so also the drive for "100
percent Americanism." First aimed at German-Americans, the
movement could be fatuous (sauerkraut was rechristened "liberty cabbage"; bars boycotted pretzels) and self-defeating
(schools banned the teaching of the German language). It could
also be vicious. In St. Louis a mob assaulted a young man for no
better reason than that he was from Germany. (Some said he
ought to be in the American military; in fact he had tried to join
the U.S. Navy but had been rejected on medical grounds.) He

was stripped, beaten, wrapped in an American flag, and hanged. The instigators of the homicide were brought to trial, but the jury was more impressed by the prowar ribbons the defendants sported than by the details of the crime. After the lawyers for the defense described the action as "patriotic murder," the jury required a mere thirty minutes to acquit. "I guess nobody can say we aren't loyal now," one proud juryman declared.[1]

Germans and German-Americans weren't the only ones targeted. Immigrants of all origins fell under suspicion, especially if their views on politics or other subjects diverged from the narrowed mainstream of American thinking. The rise of communism in Russia triggered fears that bolshevism might be coming to America, perhaps in the bags of East European immigrants. The loyalty campaign of the war years segued seamlessly into a postwar "red scare." In the autumn of 1919 the Justice Department began a roundup of leftist immigrants, many of whom were summarily deported. In January 1920 the sweep broadened, netting some four thousand Communists, fellow travelers, and unlucky individuals who merely happened to be in the vicinity when the feds descended. The ailing Wilson had next to nothing to do with these raids, which were organized and directed by Attorney General Palmer. Nor was Wilson even aware, until after the fact, of the accompanying vigilante violence against radical labor leaders, including an organizer for the Industrial Workers of the World who was hanged and mutilated by a bloodthirsty mob in Centralia, Washington. But the entire experience cast a pall over a nation already disillusioned by events directly related to the war.

Other marks of the illiberal turn in progressive thinking were less violent but more lasting. For decades opponents of alcohol had sought to ban the demon rum and its hellish equivalents, but the war added crucial elements of patriotism (doughboys must be sober, and corn diverted to whiskey production couldn't feed troops) that clinched the prohibitionists' case. The Eighteenth Amendment swept through Congress and the states, and took the nation by the throat in January 1920.

Just months later the Nineteenth Amendment, securing the vote to women, became law. By some measures this amendment reflected the expansive spirit of prewar progressivism, which had long contended that the cure for the problems of democracy was more democracy. But there was another side to the story, for many of those who supported women's suffrage did so from a belief that white, middle-class women would vote more heavily than their poorer, darker sisters and thereby neutralize the ethnic vote.

The last years of the Wilson administration also witnessed an outbreak of racial violence. Wilson hadn't helped matters by acquiescing in the adoption of segregationist policies by his subordinates, including Postmaster General Burleson. And when African-American leaders protested, he dismissed their complaints as overblown. On matters of race, Wilson was a true son of the South; his favorite movie was D. W. Griffith's elegy to the Ku Klux Klan, *The Birth of a Nation*, which Wilson reportedly called "history written with lightning."[2] Not surprisingly, when race riots broke out in East St. Louis, Missouri, in 1917, killing dozens, Wilson left the matters to locals to deal with. The violence spread, culminating in a two-week race war in Chicago in the summer of 1919 that killed thirty-eight, injured hundreds, and left thousands homeless.

After all this—in addition to the president's defeat on the Versailles treaty—it was no wonder Americans turned away from

Wilson and the Democrats and elected Warren Harding in 1920. Too ill to attend the inauguration ceremony, Wilson contented himself with a final visit to the Capitol, where his victorious enemy, Henry Cabot Lodge, informed him for the last time that the Congress was ready to adjourn. Wilson fixed Lodge with a brief glare, then said softly, "Tell them I have no further communications to make." He added, to the group, "I thank you for your courtesy."[3]

Wilson retired with Edith to a house on S Street above Dupont Circle. He talked of returning to the practice of law, and his friends humored him. But the idea went nowhere, and neither did Wilson. Visitors relieved his loneliness, drawn to him as to a relic of an era once vibrant but now forgotten. Occasionally Democrats sought to bottle the old magic: Franklin Roosevelt and others solicited money for a foundation named for Wilson and dedicated to the liberal and internationalist principles he espoused. But it was clear that they sought not his counsel but his name. "I shall try and be generous enough not to envy you," Wilson told Roosevelt.[4]

Wilson outlived Harding, who died unexpectedly in August 1923. He had himself driven to the White House for the funeral, but lacked the strength to get out of the car, and sat quietly in the vehicle while the service proceeded inside.

On the fifth anniversary of the armistice—November 11, 1923—he delivered a brief address by radio. Perhaps he reflected that this new technology, if invented a decade earlier, could have carried his voice to millions and might have made the crucial difference in the fight for the league—and spared him the crippling strain of his cross-country tour. But it was too late.

In the last week of January 1924 he suffered what Grayson diagnosed as stomach failure. Wilson understood what this meant. "The machinery is worn out," he said. "I am ready."[5] He lapsed into unconsciousness, and died on February 3, 1924.

Had Wilson died of the stroke that disabled him in October 1919, he would have died a hero, a martyr to the cause of world peace—and in the glow of appreciation, the Senate might well have ratified the Versailles treaty (perhaps with interpretive reservations). But half a decade later his idealistic vision of international order and of an American-led League of Nations seemed foolishly naive. By the judgment of most observers, Wilson had been outmaneuvered at Paris; even one member of the British delegation, John Maynard Keynes, who would become the most influential economist of the twentieth century, stormed away from the conference in disgust at what Wilson let Lloyd George and Clemenceau foist on Europe and the world. Wilson had hoped for a treaty that would transform world politics; the Versailles treaty—apart from the league, from which neither Britain nor France expected much—promised merely more of the same old politics that had produced the war in the first place. Britain and France attempted to reduce Germany to the status of a vassal, a strategy that boiled away whatever guilt the Germans felt about the war and gave them a grievance to nurse against their former antagonists and current oppressors.

Americans, meanwhile, turned even farther from Wilson's dream of enlightened involvement in world affairs. The postwar decade was the Jazz Age in America, a time of reaction against the idealism of the Progressive Era, a time when half the country took refuge in biblical literalism (convicting John Scopes of teaching evolution in Tennessee) and the other half drowned itself in bathtub gin (confirming the widespread doubts regarding prohibition). No one wanted to accept responsibility for the debacle that the war had become in the popular mind. When Wilson died, Americans mourned him respectfully for a moment, then made him a scapegoat for their collective disillusionment. Journalists and historians reexamined the American intervention in the world war and accounted it a fool's game. "We have been played for a bunch of suckers," wrote Harry Elmer Barnes in a widely endorsed indictment of Wilson's wartime diplomacy.[6]

Wilson's reputation continued to sink for several years. The stock market crash and the ensuing depression poisoned American minds toward big capitalism, while Europe's apparent descent toward another war made American isolation from that continent's conflicts an article of political faith. These two strands of skepticism wound together in congressional hearings that revealed the enormous profits arms merchants, chemical companies, and bankers had derived from the world war. When Americans thought about Wilson at all, they often perceived him as a dupe of men who knew just what they wanted from the war and used him to get it.

Only at the end of the 1930s did many Americans rediscover the virtues of Wilson's approach to world affairs. The League of Nations—handicapped from birth by America's refusal to join and by the unwillingness of the other great powers to grant it real authority—proved incapable of halting the aggression of Italy against Ethiopia, of Japan against China, and of Germany against Czechoslovakia. In each case the aggression started small and might have been averted by the kind of collective action Wilson had envisioned for the league. But the league lacked purpose and teeth, and the aggression proceeded apace.

The German invasion of Poland in 1939 converted much of Europe to Wilson's way of thinking; the Japanese attack on Pearl Harbor in 1941 brought most of America around. All of a sudden the nations fighting for their lives against the Nazis and the Japanese appreciated Wilson's central insight: that in the modern world, where the woes of any one country can quickly become the afflictions of all, idealism is sometimes the highest form of realism. The generation that succeeded Wilson had hoped to isolate America from the troubles of Europe and Asia, only to discover the hard way that isolation was no longer an option. Even as the war continued, American leaders, beginning with Wilson's Democratic protégé, Franklin Roosevelt, framed a new version of Wilson's beloved league. Roosevelt was a better politician than Wilson, having learned from Wilson's mistakes, and he took care to design the United Nations in a manner that catered to Americans' lingering distrust of foreigners. The American veto in the Security Council ensured that the United States wouldn't be compelled to act against the American national interest, traditionally defined. But the essential philosophy of the United Nations—the conviction that peace was the responsibility of all countries, that collective action was the surest guarantee against aggression, that self-government was the right of every people, that the world must find a way beyond the old anarchy to a new cooperation—was pure Wilsonianism. And when the delegates to the founding convention of the United Nations met in San Francisco in the spring of 1945 and pledged their determination "to save succeeding generations from the scourge of war," to defend the rights "of nations large and small," and to ensure "that armed force shall not be used save in the common interest," their words clearly echoed those spoken by Wilson a quarter century earlier.[7]

The United Nations disappointed many who had hoped it would banish war from the face of the earth. Some said this showed that Wilson had been wrong and that foreign policy not grounded in the realism of bloody human nature would always fail. Others said that it reflected an incomplete application of Wilson's ideals and that the very reservations that preserved the freedom of action of the United States prevented this updated league from fully achieving its—and his—goals. But no reasonable person could deny that, whatever its limitations, the new league was a force for peace. And from whatever cause, the third world war that all had feared, and many expected, never occurred.

By the late twentieth century, Wilson belonged to the world. Yet the greatest change had come over his own country. The nation that had turned away from the league in Wilson's day, and from responsibility for world order and peace, now accepted, quite matter-of-factly, its role at the center of world affairs. This was the deeper message of Wilson—and was an outcome he himself had foreseen and articulated. At his second inauguration, in March 1917, the president spoke of a transformation that was taking place in America. The German government had commenced its submarine campaign against American shipping; war clouds had gathered about the dome of the Capitol. Wilson was wise enough to dread what the war would bring but hopeful enough to discern a farther shore. He acknowledged the work left to do at home during his second term. "But we realize that the greatest things that remain to be done must be done with the whole world for stage and in cooperation with the wide and universal forces of mankind," he said. With his characteristic mix of diagnosis and prescription, he asserted that Americans were making themselves ready.

We are provincials no longer. The tragic events of the thirty months of vital turmoil through which we have just passed have made us citizens of the world. There can be no turning back. Our own fortunes as a nation are involved whether we would have it so or not.

And yet we are not the less Americans on that account. We shall be the more American if we but remain true to the principles in which we have been bred. They are not the principles of a province or of a single continent. We have known and boasted all along that they were the principles of a liberated mankind. . . .

The shadows that now lie dark upon our path will soon be dispelled, and we shall walk with the light all about us, if we be but true to ourselves—to ourselves as we have wished to be known in the counsels of the world and in the thought of all those who love liberty and justice and the right exalted.[8]

# Notes

Unless otherwise indicated, all references below are to *The Papers of Woodrow Wilson*, edited by Arthur S. Link et al., which are organized by date. Letters are from Wilson, unless otherwise noted. Full bibliographic information regarding works cited in short form is in the bibliography.

### 1. TO SEE THE BENCHES SMILE

1. Baccalaureate address, June 12, 1904.
2. Letter to Mary Peck, July 30, 1911.
3. August Heckscher, *Woodrow Wilson*, 33.
4. Draft letter to John W. Leckie, c. July 4, 1875.
5. Diary entries for June 15 and 17, 1876.
6. Letter to the *Princetonian*, Jan. 25, 1877, *Papers.*
7. *Princetonian* editorial, June 7, 1877, *Papers.*
8. Diary entry for Nov. 6, 1876.
9. Diary entry for June 16, 1876.
10. Diary entry for Nov. 10, 1876.
11. "William Earl Chatham," *Nassau Literary Magazine*, Oct. 1878, *Papers.*
12. "John Bright," *Virginia University Magazine*, Mar. 1880, *Papers.*
13. "Mr. Gladstone: A Character Sketch," *Virginia University Magazine*, Apr. 1880, *Papers.*

14. "Cabinet Government in the United States," *International Review*, Aug. 1879, *Papers*.
15. Letter to Charles A. Talcott, Dec. 31, 1879.
16. Ibid.
17. Letter from Joseph R. Wilson, Aug. 14, 1882.
18. Letter to Robert Bridges, May 24, 1881.
19. Letter to Robert Bridges, Apr. 29, 1883.
20. Letter to Robert Bridges, Nov. 19, 1884.
21. Heckscher, *Woodrow Wilson*, 76.
22. Letter to Robert Bridges, Nov. 7, 1879.
23. Heckscher, *Woodrow Wilson*, 166.
24. Arthur S. Link, *Wilson*, 1:142.
25. Letter to John M. Harlan, June 23, 1910.
26. Acceptance speech, Sept. 15, 1910.
27. News report, Sept. 17, 1910, *Papers*.
28. Statement by James Smith, Jr., Dec. 9, 1910.
29. Note to letter from James E. Martine, July 28, 1911.
30. Address, Sept. 19, 1912.
31. Address, Sept. 20, 1912.
32. Address, Sept. 23, 1912.
33. Note to address, Oct. 31, 1912.
34. Inaugural address, Mar. 4, 1913.
35. The following quotes from the exchange between Wilson and McCombs are taken from William F. McCombs, *Making Woodrow Wilson President*, edited by Louis Jay Lang (New York: Fairview, 1921), 207–9.
36. Various diary entries for 1876, for example.
37. Edward M. House, *The Intimate Papers of Colonel House*, 1:116.
38. Ibid., 1:114.
39. Letter to Edward M. House, Jan. 11, 1915.
40. Link, *Wilson*, 2:94.
41. Ibid., 152.
42. Remarks at press conference, Apr. 7, 1913.
43. Address to joint session of Congress, Apr. 8, 1913.
44. Ibid.

45. Link, *Wilson*, 2:154.
46. Statement, May 26, 1913.
47. Address to joint session, June 23, 1913.
48. Link, *Wilson*, 2:434.
49. Letter to Oscar W. Underwood, Oct. 17, 1914.

2. THE IRONY OF FATE

1. Ray Stannard Baker, ed., *Woodrow Wilson*, 4:55.
2. Statement, Mar. 12, 1913.
3. Report by William B. Hale, July 9, 1913.
4. Letter to John Lind, Aug. 4, 1913.
5. Letter to Mary A. Hulbert, Aug. 24, 1913.
6. Letter to Mary A. Hulbert, Nov. 2, 1913.
7. Link, *Wilson*, 2:391.
8. Interview, Apr. 27, 1914.
9. Address to Congress, Apr. 20, 1914.
10. Letter to William C. Adamson, July 20, 1914.
11. Link, *Wilson*, 3:481.
12. Remarks at press conference, July 27, 1914.
13. Statement, Aug. 18, 1914.
14. Letter from William Jennings Bryan, Aug. 10, 1914.
15. Letter from Robert Lansing, Sept. 6, 1915.
16. Link, *Wilson*, 3:173–74.
17. Ibid., 320.
18. *Foreign Relations of the United States*, 1915, supplement, 98–99.
19. Letter from Edward M. House, May 9, 1915.
20. Address, May 10, 1915.
21. Link, *Wilson*, 3:382.
22. Remarks at press conference, May 11, 1915.
23. *Foreign Relations of the United States*, 1915, supplement, 437–38.
24. Ibid., 481–82.
25. Letter to William Jennings Bryan, June 5, 1915.
26. Diary entry of Edward M. House, June 24, 1915.

27. Letter to William Jennings Bryan, June 9, 1915.
28. Letter to Edith Bolling Galt, Sept. 21, 1915.
29. Heckscher, *Woodrow Wilson*, 335.
30. Ibid., 340.
31. Diary entry of Edward M. House, Nov. 6, 1914.
32. Diary entry of Edward M. House, Nov. 14, 1914.
33. Heckscher, *Woodrow Wilson*, 347–48.
34. Letter to Edith Bolling Galt, May 11, 1915.
35. Letter to Edith Bolling Galt, July 20, 1915.
36. Letter from Edith Bolling Galt, June 9, 1915.
37. Link, *Wilson*, 4:229.
38. Address to Congress, Apr. 19, 1916.
39. *Foreign Relations of the United States*, 1916, supplement, 257–60.
40. Letter from Robert Lansing, May 6, 1916.
41. Heckscher, *Woodrow Wilson*, 412.

### 3. MORE PRECIOUS THAN PEACE

1. Note to letter from Edward M. House, Feb. 15, 1916.
2. Diary entry of Edward M. House, Mar. 6, 1916.
3. Address to Senate, Jan. 22, 1917.
4. Ibid.
5. Link, *Wilson*, 5:268–70.
6. Diary entry of Edward M. House, Feb. 1, 1917.
7. Address to Congress, Feb. 3, 1917.
8. Memorandum by Robert Lansing, Mar. 20, 1917.
9. Diary entry of Josephus Daniels, Mar. 20, 1917.
10. Ibid.
11. Address to Congress, Apr. 2, 1917.
12. Baker, *Woodrow Wilson*, 5:77.
13. Ibid., 7:80.
14. David M. Kennedy, *Over Here*, 112.
15. Ibid., 80.
16. H. C. Peterson and Gilbert C. Fite, *Opponents of War, 1917–1918* (Madison: University of Wisconsin Press, 1957), 22.

17. H. W. Brands, *TR: The Last Romantic* (New York: Basic Books, 1997), 781.
18. Ibid., 781–82.
19. Statement, May 18, 1917.
20. Ray Stannard Baker and William E. Dodds, eds., *The Public Papers of Woodrow Wilson*, 5:39.
21. Address to Congress, Apr. 2, 1917.
22. Kennedy, *Over Here*, 173.
23. Address to Congress, Jan. 8, 1918.
24. Ibid.
25. Address, Apr. 6, 1918.
26. Letter to Edward M. House, July 8, 1918.
27. Letter from Newton D. Baker, Nov. 27, 1918.
28. Address, Sept. 27, 1918.
29. Ibid.
30. Ibid.
31. Ibid.
32. Letter from Edward M. House, Oct. 30, 1918.
33. Ibid.
34. Statement, Nov. 11, 1918.
35. Address to Congress, Nov. 11, 1918.

## 4. WHAT WE DREAMED AT OUR BIRTH

1. Thomas J. Knock, *To End All Wars*, 169.
2. Ibid., 160.
3. Memorandum of conversation by Thomas W. Lamont, Oct. 4, 1918.
4. Knock, *To End All Wars*, 179.
5. Memorandum of conversation by Thomas W. Lamont, Oct. 4, 1918.
6. Statement, Oct. 19, 1918.
7. Knock, *To End All Wars*, 180.
8. Brands, *TR*, 809.
9. Memorandum by Frank I. Cobb, Nov. 4, 1918.

10. Knock, *To End All Wars*, 194–95.
11. Ibid., 195.
12. Address, Dec. 28, 1918.
13. Address to peace conference, Feb. 14, 1919.
14. Ibid.
15. Address, Feb. 24, 1919.
16. Remarks to Democratic National Committee, Feb. 28, 1919.
17. Address, Mar. 4, 1919.
18. H. W. Brands, *The United States in the World* (Boston: Houghton Mifflin, 1994), 2:64.
19. The following quotes from the exchange between Wilson and Clemenceau are taken from Paul Mantoux's notes of meetings, Mar. 28, 1919, and the diary entry of Edward M. House, Mar. 28, 1919.
20. Frederic William Wile, *News Is Where You Find It: Forty Years' Reporting at Home and Abroad* (Indianapolis: Bobbs-Merrill, 1939), 405.
21. After-dinner remarks, May 9, 1919.
22. Remarks, May 30, 1919.
23. Diary entry of Edward M. House, June 29, 1919.
24. Diary entry of Cary T. Grayson, July 10, 1919.
25. Address to Senate, July 10, 1919.
26. Address, Sept. 5, 1919.
27. Heckscher, *Woodrow Wilson*, 603–4.
28. Remarks, Sept. 22, 1919.
29. Remarks, Sept. 23, 1919.
30. Address, Sept. 25, 1919.
31. Phyllis Lee Levin, *Edith and Woodrow*, 295.
32. Irwin Hood Hoover, *Forty-two Years in the White House*, 99.
33. Diary entry of Cary T. Grayson, May 1, 1919.
34. Diary entry of Cary T. Grayson, Sept. 26, 1919.
35. Hoover, *Forty-two Years in the White House*, 102.
36. *Washington Post*, Oct. 6, 1919, *Papers*.
37. *New York Times*, Oct. 5, 1919, *Papers*.
38. Joseph P. Tumulty, *Woodrow Wilson as I Know Him*, 444.

39. Edith Bolling Wilson, *My Memoir,* 289.
40. Note to memorandum by Cary T. Grayson on Hitchcock inter-view, Nov. 17, 1919.
41. Memorandum by Robert Lansing, Dec. 4, 1919.

## 5. PROVINCIALS NO LONGER

1. Kennedy, *Over Here,* 68.
2. Ibid., 281.
3. Heckscher, *Woodrow Wilson,* 645.
4. Ibid., 652.
5. Cary T. Grayson, *Woodrow Wilson,* 139.
6. Quoted in H. W. Brands, *What America Owes the World: The Struggle for the Soul of Foreign Policy* (New York: Cambridge University Press, 1998), 80.
7. UN charter, preamble.
8. Second inaugural address, Mar. 5, 1917.

# Milestones

1856   Born in Staunton, Virginia (December 28)
1858   Family moves to Augusta, Georgia
1861–65   Civil War
1870   Family moves to Columbia, South Carolina
1873–74   Attends Davidson College
1874–75   Lives with family in Wilmington, North Carolina
1875–79   Attends College of New Jersey (Princeton); B.A. 1879
1877   Reconstruction terminated; last federal troops withdrawn from South
1879–80   Attends University of Virginia law school
1881–82   Reads law at home in North Carolina
1882–83   Practices law in Atlanta
1883–85   Attends graduate school at Johns Hopkins; Ph.D. 1886
1885   Publishes *Congressional Government*
      Marries Ellen Axson
1885–88   Teaches at Bryn Mawr College
1888–90   Teaches at Wesleyan University (Connecticut)
1889   Publishes *The State*
1890–1902   Teaches government at Princeton
1898   Spanish-American War
1902–10   Serves as president of Princeton
1910   Elected governor of New Jersey

1912   Defeats Theodore Roosevelt and William Howard Taft for president
1913   Underwood tariff significantly reduces rates
       Sixteenth Amendment allows federal income tax
       Seventeenth Amendment specifies direct election of senators
       Federal Reserve system established
1914   Orders landing at Vera Cruz
       First World War begins
       Ellen Wilson dies
       Panama Canal opens
       Federal Trade Commission established
1915   *Lusitania* sunk
       Extends de facto recognition to Carranza government of Mexico
       Marries Edith Bolling Galt
1916   House-Grey memorandum
       Villa attacks Columbus, New Mexico
       Orders Pershing across the Rio Grande
       *Sussex* sunk
       Narrowly defeats Charles Evans Hughes in campaign for reelection
1917   Germany launches unrestricted submarine war
       Zimmermann telegram published
       Russian Revolution begins with overthrow of czar
       Requests war declaration, which Congress grants
       Mobilization begins
       Bolsheviks seize power in Russia
1918   Delivers "Fourteen Points" speech
       Russia leaves war
       Sedition Act passed
       Orders troops to northern Russia and Siberia
       International influenza epidemic
       Urges voters to elect Democrats to Congress; voters choose Republicans

Armistice ends war
1919 Paris Peace Conference
Treaty of Versailles
Travels cross-country on behalf of treaty
Suffers debilitating stroke
Palmer raids against radicals and sympathizers
Senate rejects treaty
1920 Eighteenth Amendment takes effect, outlawing liquor
Senate rejects treaty again
Nineteenth Amendment enfranchises women
Warren Harding elected president
1924 Dies in Washington (February 3)

# Selected Bibliography

Auchincloss, Louis. *Woodrow Wilson*. New York: Viking, 2000. A brief interpretation by the novelist, critic, and all-around man of letters.

Bailey, Thomas A. *Woodrow Wilson and the Great Betrayal*. New York: Macmillan, 1945. With the next entry, an indictment of those, including Wilson, who threw away the chance for a League of Nations that might have prevented the war under way at the time the author wrote.

———. *Woodrow Wilson and the Lost Peace*. New York: Macmillan, 1944.

Baker, Ray Stannard, ed. *Woodrow Wilson: Life and Letters*. 8 vols. Garden City, N.Y.: Doubleday, Page, 1927–39. Wilson's most avid admirer among progressive journalists re-creates the life of the great man. Includes interviews with many Wilson contemporaries.

Blum, John M. *Woodrow Wilson and the Politics of Morality*. Boston: Little, Brown, 1956. An elegant biographical essay by an insightful historian of the Progressive Era.

Bragdon, Henry Wilkinson. *Woodrow Wilson: The Academic Years*. Cambridge, Mass.: Belknap Press of Harvard University Press, 1967. Before he descended the ivory tower.

Clements, Kendrick A. *The Presidency of Woodrow Wilson*. Lawrence, Kans.: University Press of Kansas, 1992. The eight years in office.

————. *Woodrow Wilson: World Statesman*. Boston: Twayne, 1987. A succinct life.

Cooper, John Milton, Jr. *Breaking the Heart of the World: Woodrow Wilson and the Fight for the League of Nations*. Cambridge, England, and New York: Cambridge University Press, 2001. The most thorough postmortem.

————. *The Warrior and the Priest: Woodrow Wilson and Theodore Roosevelt*. Cambridge, Mass.: Belknap Press of Harvard University Press, 1983. A comparative study of the towering political figures of their era.

Ferrell, Robert H. *Woodrow Wilson and World War I, 1917–1921*. New York: Harper and Row, 1985. A distinguished diplomatic historian examines Wilson's wartime diplomacy.

Gardner, Lloyd C. *Safe for Democracy: The Anglo-American Response to Revolution, 1913–1923*. New York: Oxford University Press, 1984. Wilsonian diplomacy in transatlantic context.

George, Alexander L., and Juliette L. George. *Woodrow Wilson and Colonel House: A Personality Study*. New York: J. Day, 1956. In a genre—psychohistory—characterized by armchair diagnosis and unexamined assumptions, an atypically careful and illuminating work.

Grayson, Cary T. *Woodrow Wilson: An Intimate Memoir*. New York: Holt, Rinehart, and Winston, 1960. The doctor speaks, guardedly.

Heckscher, August. *Woodrow Wilson*. New York: Charles Scribner's Sons, 1991. The finest single-volume biography. Sympathetic but objective.

Hoover, Herbert. *The Ordeal of Woodrow Wilson*. New York: McGraw-Hill, 1958. By one who knew him, and who knew what an ordeal the presidency could be.

Hoover, Irwin Hood (Ike). *Forty-two Years in the White House*. Boston: Houghton Mifflin, 1934. What the butler saw.

House, Edward M. *The Intimate Papers of Colonel House, Arranged as a Narrative by Charles Seymour*. Ed. Charles Seymour. 4 vols. Boston: Houghton Mifflin, 1926–28. The president's confidant has his say. Includes accounts of conversations unavailable else-where, albeit filtered through the alter ego.

Kennedy, David M. *Over Here: The First World War and American Society.* New York: Oxford University Press, 1980. The best account of Wilson's America during wartime.

Kissinger, Henry. *Diplomacy.* New York: Simon and Schuster, 1994. Amid much else, an explanation of Wilson's lasting influence on foreign affairs, and a critique of same.

Knock, Thomas J. *To End All Wars: Woodrow Wilson and the Quest for a New World Order.* New York: Oxford University Press, 1992. A penetrating analysis of Wilson's approach to foreign policy.

Levin, N. Gordon, Jr. *Woodrow Wilson and World Politics: America's Response to War and Revolution.* New York: Oxford University Press, 1968. The ideology of Wilsonianism, critically rendered.

Levin, Phyllis Lee. *Edith and Woodrow: The Wilson White House.* New York: Scribner, 2001. An exposé of the conspiracy surrounding Wilson's illness.

Link, Arthur S. *Wilson.* 5 vols. Princeton: Princeton University Press, 1947–65. A labor of love by Wilson's biggest fan. Enormous detail on how Wilson became president and what he did during his first four and a half years; but rather less than complete objectivity.

Tumulty, Joseph P. *Woodrow Wilson as I Know Him.* Garden City, N.Y.: Doubleday, Page, 1921. An apology for the invalid by his political man Friday.

Walworth, Arthur. *Wilson and His Peacemakers: American Diplomacy at the Paris Peace Conference.* New York: Norton, 1986. How making peace is harder than making war.

Weinstein, Edwin A. *Woodrow Wilson: A Medical and Psychological Biography.* Princeton: Princeton University Press, 1981. A judicious and revealing account of how Wilson's body failed him, and what that did to his mind.

Wilson, Edith Bolling. *My Memoir.* Indianapolis: Bobbs-Merrill, 1939. Handle with care.

Wilson, Woodrow, *The Papers of Woodrow Wilson.* Ed. Arthur S. Link et al. 69 vols. Princeton: Princeton University Press, 1966–94. The man of words in all their glory. Link's monument to his hero; beautifully compiled, edited, and annotated.

———. *The Public Papers of Woodrow Wilson.* Ed. Ray Stannard Baker and William E. Dodd. 6 vols. New York: Harper and Brothers, 1925–27. Includes material not reproduced in *The Papers of Woodrow Wilson.*

———. *Congressional Government: A Study in American Politics.* Boston: Houghton, Mifflin, 1885. Still worth a look.

## SUGGESTIONS FOR FURTHER READING

The reader wishing to know more about Wilson the man might start with August Heckscher's biography, which gives Wilson his due without sacrificing historical detachment. The Wilson presidency is surveyed capably by Kendrick Clements. Arthur Link's five volumes offer much more detail than Clements's one, but little searching analysis of Wilson, and they carry the story only up to American entry into the world war. Robert Ferrell supplies the best introduction to Wilson's wartime diplomacy, while John Milton Cooper (*Breaking the Heart of the World*) and Thomas Knock focus on Paris and after, and on the mind of Wilson. Other titles annotated above deal with particular aspects of the man and his career. But no reader who really wants to know Wilson should neglect his own writings, which are marvelously presented by Link and associates in *The Papers of Woodrow Wilson.*

# Index

ABC solution, 49
Adams, John, 29
African-American leaders, 133
alcohol, 132–33
Allied Powers, 52
  U.S. loans to, 56
Allies, 74, 75, 88, 97, 101, 105
  casualties, 94
  moral case for intervention on
    side of, 79
  secret treaties, 88
  submarine problem, 58
  winning, 93
America
  system of governance, 12, 51
  transformation in, 138–39
  Wilson on, 22, 60
  see also United States
American cause, 95–96
American Expeditionary Force,
  94
American leadership
  death of Wilson's dream of,
    130
American Revolution, 114

American ships
  sinking of, 79, 119
  stopped and boarded, 57
  submarine campaign and, 58–59,
    138
American troops, 87–88, 93
  what they fought for, 105,
    117–18
Americans/American people
  expectations of League of
    Nations, 114
  and foreign affairs, 133–34,
    135–36
  killed in submarine attacks, 59,
    61, 69–70, 79
  support for treaty and League of
    Nations, 116–22
  Wilson's appeal to, regarding
    League of Nations, 117–18,
    130
  and World War I, 52–53, 63,
    68, 71
Anglophilia, 29
antimonopoly measures, 38–39
antitrust law, revision of, 36–38

antitrust prosecution, 27
 suspension of, 83
*Arabic* (passenger vessel), 69
*Arabic* pledge, 69
Argentina, 48–49
armistice, 97, 99
 Fourteen Points basis for, 97–98
arms control, 75
arms merchants, 54, 136
association of nations (proposed),
 89
Augusta, Georgia, 2
Austria, 56
Austria-Hungary, 52
Austrian empire, 115

Baker, Newton, 88, 92
Baker, Ray Stannard, 82
balance of power, 76, 105
Balfour, Arthur, 97, 102
Bank of the United States
 second, 34
banking system, 35–36, 37, 38
banks, 56
 private, 34–35
Barnes, Harry Elmer, 136
Belgium, German invasion of, 53
Belleau Wood, 93
Bernstorff, Johann, 69
biblical literalism, 135
big business, 20–21, 23, 31
Big Four, 115
big government, 82
*Birth of a Nation, The* (film), 133
blockades, 56–58, 71, 77
Bolsheviks/bolshevism, 88, 91, 132
Borah, William, 121
Brahany, Thomas, 85–86

Brandeis, Louis, 27, 35, 37
Brazil, 48–49
Brest Litovsk, 90
 dictated peace of, 91
Bright, John, 7, 8
Britain/British
 and American troops, 87–88
 blockade, 56, 57, 58, 71, 77
 and Bolshevik coup, 91, 92
 empire, 105, 112, 115
 and League of Nations, 116
 loans to, 55
 and peace conference, 74, 105,
 111, 112–14, 135
 and peace proposal, 90, 94, 97
 trade with, in World War I, 56
 World War I, 52, 53, 56, 60, 69,
 88, 93
British Isles
 war zone around, 58, 77
British system of governance
 Wilson's enthusiasm for,
 29, 51
Bryan, William Jennings, 15, 20,
 25–26, 35, 54–55, 56, 60
 Wilson's break with, 62–63,
 66, 67
Bryanism, 16
Bryn Mawr, 11
bully pulpit, 20
Burke, Edmund, 7
Burleson, Albert Sidney, 26, 133
business
 and Wilson, 37–38
 *see also* big business

California, 121–22
Carnegie, Andrew, 14

Carranza, Venustiano, 44, 49,
    50–51
central bank, 34–35
Central Powers, 52, 92, 95, 117
    U.S. loans to, 56
Centralia, Washington, 132
Châtaeu-Thierry, 93
Chile, 48–49
China, 136
Civil War, 2, 3, 15, 51
Clark, Champ, 20, 24, 30, 84
Clayton, Henry, 36
Clayton bill, 36–37, 38
Clemenceau, Georges, 90, 94, 102,
    103, 104
    and peace conference, 111–14,
    115, 116, 118, 135
Cleveland, Grover, 15
Cobb, Frank, 103
collective action, 136, 137
collective security, guarantee of,
    106, 108, 128
College of New Jersey (Princeton),
    5–6, 8
    became Princeton, 13
colonial claims, adjustment of, 89
Columbia University, 14
Columbus, Ohio, 120
commander in chief, Wilson as, 81
Committee on Public Information
    (CPI), 82, 84
communism, 132
Congress, 7–8, 11, 15, 38, 48, 127
    controlled by other party, 101
    and declaration of war, 74, 81
    passage of Eighteenth
    Amendment, 133
    Republican control of, 99, 107

tariff reduction, 33
    and taxes, 83
    Wilson addressing, 29–31, 35, 36,
    70, 78, 79–80, 88–89, 98, 134
    Wilson and, 71
    see also House of
    Representatives; Senate
congressional elections, 38, 111
    referendum on Wilson's handling
    of war, 99–103
Congressional Government
    (Wilson), 11
conscription, 85, 87
conservatives
    opposition to League of Nations,
    116–17
Constitution, 29
    Eighteenth Amendment, 127,
    133
    Nineteenth Amendment, 133
    Sixteenth Amendment, 34
constitutionalism, 43–44
Constitutionalists (Mexico), 44,
    47, 49, 50
contraband, 54, 56–57
Creel, George, 82
Croly, Herbert, 100
Czechoslovakia/Czechs, 92, 136

Daniels, Josephus, 26, 79, 81
Davidson College, 4–5
Davis, Jefferson, 2
debates, 7–8
Debs, Eugene, 84
democracy, 17, 80, 133
    in Mexico, 47
Democratic National Committee,
    109

Democratic party/Democrats, 6–7,
    15–17, 37, 130, 134
    election of 1912, 1, 19–20
    and vote on treaty, 129, 130
    and Wilson election to New
        Jersey governorship, 18–19
    Wilson's relationship with,
        23–24, 32
depressions, 34, 136
Diaz, Porfirio, 42
diplomacy, 70, 71, 73–78
    idealism, in, 131
    in postwar settlement, 94
    wartime, 136
domestic issues
    in 1916 campaign, 68
Dominican Republic, 50

East St. Louis, Missouri, 133
economy (the), government and,
    34, 35, 36
education, politics and, 13–14
Eighteenth Amendment, 127, 133
electoral college, 23
Eliot, Charles, 14
England
    statesmen and orators of, 7
    see also Britain/British
Espionage Act, 84, 100, 131
estate taxes, 83
Ethiopia, 136
Europe
    territorial settlements, 89
    war in, 51–52, 68
    Wilson's reception in, 104
    and World War II, 136–37
excess-profits tax, 83

excise taxes, 31, 83
executive branch, 8, 30
executive leadership, new style
    of, 31

Falaba (liner), 59
federal agencies and offices,
    82–83
federal power, dark side of, 84
Federal Reserve Act, 35–36
Federal Reserve system, 36
Federal Trade Commission, 38,
    82, 83
federal trade commission
    (proposed), 37–38
financial panics, 34
Fiume, 115
Foch, Ferdinand, 104
foreign affairs, 26, 41–63
    American people and, 133–34,
        135–36
foreign policy, 45, 91–93, 108,
    137–38
    cardinal tenets of, 109–10
Fourteen Points, 89, 94–95
    as basis for armistice, 97–98
France
    and American troops, 87
    and Bolshevik coup, 91, 92
    empire, 115
    and League of Nations, 116
    loans to, 54, 55
    and peace conference, 74, 105,
        111, 112–14, 135
    and peace proposal, 94, 97
    trade with, in World War I, 56
    World War I, 52, 87, 88, 93

Franco-Prussian War of 1870–71, 51
freedom of the seas, 57, 75, 89

George Washington (ship), 104, 107, 108, 115
German-Americans, 131–32
Germany, 85, 122
    accountability and reparations, 105, 112
    blockade by, 58
    empire, 115
    France demanding Saar region of, 113, 116
    and peace proposal, 90, 94–95
    proposed alliance with Mexico and Japan, 78
    reparations bill against, 116
    sued for armistice, 97
    trade with, in World War I, 56
    U.S. ultimatum to, 70–71, 73–74
    vassal status in treaty, 135
    in World War I, 52, 53, 57, 69, 75, 90–91, 93
    World War I: submarine campaign, 58–60, 61–62, 69–71, 73, 77–78, 80, 138
    World War I: torpedoing American ships, 79
    World War II, 136
Gladstone, William, 7, 8
government, American system of, 12, 51
    role in economy, 34, 35, 36
    theory of, 12
Grayson, Cary, 64, 65, 66, 123–24, 125–26, 134

Gregory, Thomas, 83, 84
Grey, Edward, 74
Giffith, D. W., 133
Gulflight (tanker), 59

Haiti, 50
Hale, William Bayard, 44
Harding, Warren, 134
Harper's Weekly, 14, 19
Harvard University, 14
Harvey, George, 14, 16, 19
Hayes, R. B., 6, 7
Hays, Will, 102
History of the American People (Wilson), 14
Hitchcock, Gilbert, 129
Hoover, Ike, 123, 125
Hopkins, Johns, 11
Howe, Edward, 59–60, 62, 77, 85, 92, 97, 101, 103
    adviser to Wilson, 27–28
    end to Wilson's relationship with, 111
    friendship with Wilson, 64–65
    and League of Nations, 118
    and peace conference, 111–12
    sent to England, 74
    threatened by presence of Edith Wilson, 67–68
    and World War I, 68, 69
    House-Grey memorandum, 74–75
House of Representatives, 30
    Democratic control of, 23, 24
Huerta, Victoriano, 42, 43, 44, 46–47, 48–49

Hughes, Charles Evans, 71, 72, 86, 100
human nature, 10, 112, 113, 138

Idaho, 121
idealism
  embodied in League of Nations, 117
  highest form of realism, 137
  reaction against, 131, 135
  of Wilson, 81, 108, 113, 115, 129, 135, 138
immigrants, 132
import taxes
  *see* tariffs
income tax, 34
  shift from tariff to, 83
Indiana, 120–21
Industrial Workers of the World, 84, 132
industrial production
  World War I, 83
international affairs
  *see* foreign affairs
international law, 52, 54
international order, Wilson's view of, 135
*International Review*, 7
internationalism, 100, 108, 134
isolation, 136, 137
Italy, 136

J. P. Morgan and Company, 54
Jackson, Andrew, 34
Japan
  attack on Pearl Harbor, 136
  preparing to invade Russia, 91, 92

proposed alliance with Germany, 78
World War II, 137
Jazz Age, 135
Jefferson, Thomas, 29
Johns Hopkins, 11, 12
Justice Department, 27, 84, 132
justice for all (principle), 89

Keynes, John Maynard, 135
Ku Klux Klan, 28, 133

La Follette, Robert, 76
Lansing, Robert, 56, 68, 69, 71, 79, 85, 103, 125, 126, 127
  resignation, 129–30
Latin America, 45, 48
League of Nations, 100, 103, 108, 126, 135
  amendment to proposed charter, 114
  charter covenant, 121–22, 128
  draft charter, 106–7
  draft charter: Article Ten, 106–7, 116, 128
  opposition to, in U.S., 116–17, 127–28
  weakness of, 136
  Wilson's work for, 105–6, 107, 108–11, 112, 114–22
League of Nations (proposed), 96–97
"League of Peace" (proposed), 75–76
Lenin, Nikolai, 88, 91
liberals, 100
  opposition to League of Nations, 116–17

Lind, John, 45–46
Lloyd George, David, 94, 103, 104,
  112, 116, 118
  and peace conference, 111–13,
    115, 116, 135
Lodge, Henry Cabot, 107–10, 116,
  117, 119, 128, 129, 134
  opposed treaty, 107, 117,
    118–19
  treaty reservations, 127–28, 130
Low, Seth, 14
loyalty campaign, 132
Lusitania (liner), sinking of, 59–60,
  61–62, 66, 68, 69

Madero, Francisco, 42, 43, 44
Marne, 93
Marshall, Thomas, 125
McAdoo, William, 26
McCombs, William, 24–25
merchant vessels, submarines
  attacking, 71
Mexico, 42–50
  proposed alliance with Germany,
    78
  revolution, 44, 49, 50
  U.S. invasion of Vera Cruz,
    48–49
Mexico City, 49, 51
military draft, 84–85, 87
Missouri, 120–21
money supply, 34
  control of, 35
money trust, 34–36
monopolies, 31, 36, 39
Monroe, James, 45
Monroe Doctrine, 45, 109, 114
Montana, 121

Morgan, J. P., 14
muckrakers, 14, 20, 82

Napoleon, defeat of, 51
Nation, 100
national interest (U.S.), 54, 137
Nazis, 137
neutral rights, 59, 60, 62, 80
neutrality (U.S.), 52–53, 54, 56, 62,
  79
neutrals (World War I)
  and submarine campaign, 58
  trading rights, 57
New Freedom, 23, 36, 68, 82, 83,
  128
New Jersey governorship
  Wilson and, 16–19, 27
New Nationalism, 23, 82, 128
New Republic, 77
New York Law School, 12
New York Times, 77, 121
Nineteenth Amendment, 133
nonentanglement policy, 109
nonrecognition policy, 44, 45
Nugent, James, 19

Ogden, Utah, 122
"100 percent Americanism,"
  131–32
oratory, 7, 29
Orlando, Vittorio, 115
Ottoman empire, 89, 115
Ottoman Turkey, 52

pacifism, 26, 54, 81
Palmer, A. Mitchell, 84, 132
Panama Canal, 41
Paris, 104, 105

party primaries, 19
passenger ships
    attacked by submarines, 69–70
peace
    basis of, 76
    collective responsibility for, 106,
        137
    principle for, 89–90
    without victory, 75
    Wilson's efforts for, 77, 80, 88
peace conference, 73–77, 120
    postwar, 88
    Wilson attending, 103–7,
        111–16, 123, 124, 135
peace program (U.S.)
    Fourteen Points, 89–90, 94–95,
        97–98
peacekeeping efforts (U.S.),
    94–98
Pearl Harbor, 136
Peck, Mary, 63
Pershing, John, 50, 87–88, 94, 98
Philippines, 41
philosophical difference
    Wilson/Europeans, 112–13
Pinchot, Amos, 100
Pitt, William, 7
Poland, 136
political corruption, 31–32
politics
    in decision regarding World
        War I, 70, 135
    and education, 13–14
    international, 96–97
    of ratification, 129
    structure of, 15
    Wilson and/on, 6–7, 8, 10, 17,
        19, 29, 73, 81, 101

presidency
    Republicans holding, 15
    Wilson candidate for, 16, 17
presidency (Wilson), 23–39
    advisers in, 27–29
    appointments, 26
    end of, 130
    international affairs, 41–63
    state of the union message
        hallmark of, 30–31
    and World War I, 51–63, 68–78
presidential campaign(s), 6–7,
    19–23, 24
    for reelection, 68, 71–72
presidential elections
    Democrats in, 15
Princeton, 5–6, 8
    Wilson's career at, 11, 12–13,
        14–15, 17
principles
    American, 139
    for peace, 89–90
    Wilson, 73, 76
Progressive (Bull Moose) party, 19
Progressive Era, 135
progressives/progressivism, 13–14,
    18, 44, 45
    and antitrust law, 36–37
    in election of 1912, 20
    legislation, 71
    perverted, 131–33
    and tariffs, 31–32
    in tax structure, 34
    and war, 81–82
    and war as engine of tax reform,
        83
    Wilson as, 43, 112
prohibition, 127, 133, 135

public speaking, 4, 6
Pueblo, Colorado, 122
"Punitive Expedition," 50

racial violence, 133
recession (1913), 37
Reconstruction, 2
"red scare," 133
reelection, 72, 73
reform(s), 24, 82
religion, 25
Renick and Wilson (law firm), 10
reparations, 105, 112
reparations bill, 116
Republican Party/Republicans, 19,
    24
  control of Congress, 99, 102, 107
  opposed League of Nations, 110,
    116, 117, 121
  opposition to treaty, 127–28
  and the war, 99, 102, 103
rhetoric, 5–6
Rockefeller, John D., 36
Rome, 104, 105
Roosevelt, Franklin D., 26, 134,
    137
Roosevelt, Theodore, 3, 7, 19, 37,
    71, 73, 81
  campaign of 1912, 20–21,
    22, 23
  corollary to Monroe Doctrine,
    45, 47–48
  criticism of Wilson's war aims,
    100
  death of, 107
  on defeat of Democrats, 102–3
  idea for volunteer division,
    85–87

New Nationalism, 23, 82, 128
progressivism, 13–14
Roosevelt [T.] administration, 36
Roosevelt Corollary, 47–48
Root, Elihu, 14
Rough Riders, 85
Russia, 52
  communism in, 152
  Germany imposed victor's peace
    on, 90
  intervention in, 91–93
  revolution, 78–79, 92
Russian Revolution, 88

Sacramento, 121–22
St. Louis, 121, 131
Scopes, John, 135
Scott, Walter, 5
secession, 2
Sedition Act of 1918, 84, 100, 131
segregationist policies, 133
self-determination, 115
self-government, 75, 137
Senate, 30
  Democratic control of, 23
  Foreign Relations Committee,
    108, 120
  and League of Nations, 114, 116,
    117, 118–19, 128–29
  treaty defeated in, 129, 130,
    135
Shafroth, John, 76–77
Sherman Act of 1890, 36
shorthand, 3–4, 5
Siberia, 92–93
Sixteenth Amendment, 34
slavery, 2
Smith, James, 16, 19

South (the), 19, 28
  stronghold of Democrats, 15, 16
  Wilson son of, 1, 6, 133
Spain, 85
Spanish-American War of 1898,
  41, 81, 85
speeches/speaking tours, 19, 33
  campaign for New Jersey
    governorship, 17–18
  campaign of 1912, 21–23
  state of the union, 29–31
  for treaty and League of Nations,
    120–22
Standard Oil Company, 36
State, The (Wilson), 12
State Department, 42–43, 45, 54,
  78
state of the union address, 29–31
statesmen
  Wilson admired, 7, 8
Staunton, Ohio, 2
stock market crash of 1929, 36, 136
submarine warfare, 58–60, 61–62,
  69–71, 73, 77–78, 138
Suresnes Cemetery, 117–18
Sussex (ferry), 69, 70, 73, 74
Sussex pledge, 71

Taft, William Howard, 19, 22, 23,
  110, 114
Taft administration, 36, 47
Tampico, 48
Tarbell, Ida, 82
tariffs, 31–34, 37, 38
  shift from, to income tax, 83
tax regime, 83
tax structure, revising, 31–34
territorial settlements, 89

Tilden, Samuel, 6–7
trade
  dismantling of barriers to, 89
trade, wartime, 56–57
  with belligerents, 55–56
  blockades and, 57
treaties, secret, 88–89
treaties, ratification of, 128
Treaty of Versailles, 109–10, 112,
  116, 117
  defeated in Senate, 129–30
  opposition to, 127
  reservations, 127–28, 129, 130,
    135, 138
  signed, 116
  Wilson refused to compromise
    on, 128–29
  Wilson trying to get approved in
    U.S., 109–10, 116–22
  Wilson's defeat on, 133
Trenton True American, 17, 18
trusts, 20–21, 29, 36–39
  money trust, 34–36
  tariffs and, 31
Tumulty, Joseph, 28–29, 86, 124,
  125–26, 127
Twain, Mark, 14

Underwood, Oscar, 32–33
unfair trade practices, 36, 37
United Nations, 137–38
  Security Council, 137
United States
  breaking diplomatic relations
    with Germany, 78
  declaration of war, 80–81
  as economic power in World
    War I, 53–54, 56

freedom of action, 138
international role of, 138
invasion of Vera Cruz, 48–49
loans to belligerents in World
  War I, 54–56
and Mexico, 42, 45–46, 47, 49,
  50
neutrality in World War I, 52–53,
  54, 56, 62, 79
program of peace, 89–90, 94–95,
  97–98
protests against blockades, 57–58
troops sent to Mexico, 50
ultimatum to Germany, 70–71,
  73–74
and/in World War I, 51–63,
  70–71, 73–74, 76–78, 79,
  80–83, 84, 87–88, 93–94, 100,
  119, 136
University of Illinois, 12
University of Virginia, 8–9, 13

Vera Cruz, 48
Villa, Francisco (Pancho), 47, 49,
  50
Volstead Act, 127
volunteer divisions, 87
volunteers, 84–85

Wall Street, 27
war, hope to banish, 137
War Department, 84
war effort, 82–83, 84
War Industries Board (WIB), 83
war production, logistics of, 83
Washington, Booker T., 14
Washington, George, 29, 31
weapons reduction, 89

Wesleyan College, 11
West, Andrew, 14–15, 26
Whiskey Rebellion, 31
Wilhelm, Kaiser, 53
Williams, John, 29
Wilson, Edith Bolling Galt, 65–68,
  111, 112, 134
advising Wilson, 67, 101
role in disposition of public
  affairs, 126–27, 129
and Wilson's strokes, 125,
  126–27
Wilson, Ellen Axson, 63–64, 65,
  66, 68
Wilson, Henry Lane, 44
Wilson, Joseph, 2, 3, 4, 5, 9, 10, 11
Wilson, Thomas Woodrow
academic career, 11, 12–15
birth, early life, 2–4
death of, 131, 134–35, 136
dyslexia, 3, 123
education, 3–6
education: studying law, 8–10
effect of first wife's death on,
  64–65
forebears, 1–2
illness, 122–27, 128, 129, 132,
  234
intuition, 64
lack of friends, 26, 28, 64
law career, 10
legacy of, in words, 1
message of, 138–39
personal characteristics,
  2–3, 63
reputation, 136
as speaker, 17–18, 19, 30, 103
strokes, 123–27

Wilson administration
    last years of, 133
    protesting blockade, 57
    and *Lusitania* affair, 59–62
Wilsonianism, 137
women's suffrage, 133
words, 3
    and power, 8
    Wilson man of, 1
    Wilson's way with, 60–61, 71,
        72, 177
World War I, 33–34, 51–63, 68–78,
    90–91
    American intervention in, 136
    Congressional elections
        referendum on Wilson's
        handling of, 99–103

    effect on reforming spirit in
        America, 131
    U.S. and/in, 51–63, 70–71,
        73–74, 76–78, 79, 80–83,
        84, 87–88, 92–94, 100,
        119, 136
    U.S. declaration of war,
        80–81
    U.S. neutrality in, 52–53, 54,
        56, 62, 79
    and Wilson's reelection, 68
World War II, 136–37
writing, 5–6, 10

Zapata, Emiliano, 44, 49
Zapatistas, 49
Zimmermann, Arthur, 78

# ABOUT THE AUTHOR

H. W. Brands is a distinguished professor of history and holder of the Melbern G. Glasscock Chair at Texas A&M University. His previous books include the Pulitzer Prize finalist *The First American: The Life and Times of Benjamin Franklin, The Age of Gold,* and *TR,* a biography of Theodore Roosevelt. He lives in Austin, Texas.